THE EXILE AND BEYOND

Smyth & Helwys Publishing, Inc.
6316 Peake Road
Macon, Georgia 31210-3960
1-800-747-3016
©2014 by Smyth & Helwys Publishing
All rights reserved.
Printed in the United States of America.

The paper used in this publication meets the minimum requirements of
American National Standard for Information Sciences—
Permanence of Paper for Printed Library Materials.
ANSI Z39.48–1984. (alk. paper)

Library of Congress Cataloging-in-Publication Data

Ballard, Harold Wayne, 1963-
The exile and beyond / by H. Wayne Ballard, Jr.
pages cm
ISBN 978-1-57312-759-2 (pbk. : alk. paper)
1. Bible. Old Testament--Criticism, interpretation, etc.
2. Jews--History--586 B.C.-70 A.D. I. Title.
BS1171.3.B35 2015
224'.06--dc23

2014045298

The Exile and Beyond

H. Wayne Ballard, Jr.

Dedicated to the Memory of Marvin E. Tate & Page H. Kelley
Professors, Christian Statesmen, Mentors, & Friends

Contents

Acknowledgements — vii

Introduction
The Exile and Beyond — 1

Chapter 1
Ezekiel — 5

Chapter 2
Isaiah — 31

Chapter 3
Haggai — 47

Chapter 4
Zechariah — 55

Chapter 5
Malachi — 69

Chapter 6
1 & 2 Chronicles — 79

Chapter 7
Ezra/Nehemiah — 101

Chapter 8
Joel — 119

Chapter 9
Jonah — 129

Chapter 10
Song of Songs — 143

Chapter 11
Esther — 157

Chapter 12
Daniel — 171

Acknowledgements

I would like to personally thank Keith Gammons, the editor who first approached me with the offer to write this volume for the *All the Bible* series. Over the years, Keith has proven to be a person of great patience and encouragement. Thanks, Keith, for affording me this opportunity.

It is a true honor to help complete the *All the Bible* series. Two of its first contributors are heroes of mine. Page H. Kelley wrote *Journey to the Land of Promise: Genesis–Deuteronomy* just before he died. Marvin E. Tate wrote *From Promise to Exile: The Former Prophets*. These two men personally served as mentors to me during my educational pilgrimage while completing a Ph.D. at The Southern Baptist Theological Seminary during a time of political turmoil and upheaval. Both of these men became much more than just professors to me. They were friends, encouragers, and Christian statesmen in a time and place where it was often extremely difficult to maintain one's personal walk with Christ.

I would also like to thank Dr. Randall O'Brien and Dr. Kina Mallard, president and provost at Carson-Newman University. I have been able to finish this manuscript during a recent sabbatical leave. Without this release time the final completion of this manuscript might never have come to pass. Of course, a thanks is also due to my colleagues in the department of religion at Carson-Newman, who constantly challenge me to be more Christ-like in my personal walk and teaching each and every day. Dr. Christine Jones is especially due a word of thanks for her extra help in proofreading part of this manuscript.

I want to thank my lovely wife of the past twenty-nine years, Kim Ballard. She has constantly encouraged me to be the person God has called me to be, regardless of the costs. When we were first married, I asked her to leave her family in Oklahoma and embark on a journey that we never thought possible. She never looked back!

Finally, to you the reader, I hope you find something in this work that encourages you in your personal journey of faith. Whether in matters of agreement or disputation, I hope you find these words uplifting and useful in your own study of the postexilic texts of the Old Testament.

Respectfully,

H. Wayne Ballard, Jr.
Strawberry Plains, Tennessee

Introduction

The Exile and Beyond

Second Kings 25 and 2 Chronicles 36 are perhaps two of the saddest chapters in the entirety of the Old Testament. These two chapters describe in a simple narrative fashion the devastation and apparent ending of the great promise the God of Israel made to Abraham. There is such a note of defeat permeating these texts. What began with such promise, such opportunity, has now been laid to waste. The stories of hope and inspiration found in the tales of the patriarchs, the conquest, and the establishment of the monarchy must have seemed so far away at this moment in history to the people of Judah. Nebuchadnezzar and the Babylonians have wiped out the city of Jerusalem, the temple, and the hopes and dreams of an entire nation.

With this simple act the exile has begun—an age where the elite of Judah who survived the atrocities described in the book of Lamentations were driven from the land of promise to a foreign land where they lived as political prisoners of the great Babylonian Empire. Many of the leaders of Judah were simply killed. Those left behind had no one to lead them, to encourage them, or to show them a way out of their newfound predicament. There was little or no hope.

Sometimes in our world there are many who find themselves in a similar situation. The loss of a job, the breakup of a relationship or marriage, terrible news of a newly discovered illness, or a host of other maladies can invade our lives. We, too, live among people who are enduring their own personal "exiles" every day. In my own life, the past fourteen years have been a time of deep soul searching and trial. On May 7, 2000, my youngest son, Henderson Jake Ballard, died in his sleep in the church nursery of Buies Creek First Baptist Church in Buies Creek, North Carolina. What had begun with such promise—a sweet, loving child filled with energy and enthusiasm—was now forever gone.

Second Chronicles 36, unlike its companion text in 2 Kings 25, brings a flicker of light into an otherwise dark cavern of hopelessness for the remnant of the nation of Judah. The author of 2 Kings 25 offers a comforting word, describing the release of King Jehoiachin after a thirty-seven-year period of exile and captivity, but this does little to lessen the misfortune of the people who were still suffering the effects of either living in foreign captivity or living in their homeland with inadequate leadership. Approximately sixty years after the first captives were taken into Babylon along with their king, the king of Persia, Cyrus, issued the following decree: "The LORD, the God of heaven, has given me all the kingdoms of the earth and he has appointed me to build a temple for him at Jerusalem in Judah. Any of his people among you may go up, and may the LORD their God be with them" (2 Chron 36:23 NIV).

With these simple words a flame of hope flickers anew. Cyrus allowed the captured people of Judah to return home. As indicated in the biblical texts, many people decided to remain in Babylon to continue with the new lives they had created in this foreign land. For those who did return to Palestine and Jerusalem, what they encountered when they returned was most disheartening and disappointing. The stories they had been told by their parents and grandparents of better days in Judah were juxtaposed to the stark realities they encountered upon their return. The returning exiles found their ancestral homeland in a state of waste without any legitimate leadership to rebuild those things destroyed by the Babylonians. The land of promise had become a land of misery and helplessness. Isaiah 64:10 describes the scene: "Your sacred cities have

Introduction: The Exile and Beyond

become a wasteland; even Zion is a wasteland, Jerusalem a desolation" (NIV). With these simple words a new era had begun for the people of Israel and Judah, the time of restoration and hope, a time sometimes described by scholars as the postexilic period.

It is the intent of this volume to bring to life the sacred literature of Israel and Judah that comprise the writings of the exilic and postexilic communities of faith. Though life brings periods of trial at various points in our lives, we are also challenged with how we respond to the obstacles that lay before us. Will we choose to live the remainder our days in the land of exile, or will we return to our ancestral homelands and take up the challenge of rebuilding our lives into something new and fresh? In this volume we will experience the exile through the eyes of Ezekiel, who, along with the first wave of deportees and King Jehoiachin, was taken into Babylon around the year 598 BCE. Deutero and Trito Isaiah describe life in the exile with hope of the promised return under the watchful eye of Cyrus, the Persian king. Haggai, Zechariah, and Malachi instruct us on the conditions encountered by those who chose to return to Palestine and rebuild Jerusalem and the temple following the decree of Cyrus. Ezra and Nehemiah offer a further glimpse into the world of those refugees who had built considerable stations for themselves in their "new" homeland but chose to forego this life of privilege in order to return to their ancestral home and aid in the rebuilding. First and Second Chronicles provide a retrospective of Israel's history from the vantage point of surviving the exile, demonstrating how the ancient story of Israel can be interpreted in light of devastation and loss. Daniel, Jonah, and Esther represent very late works in the writing of the Old Testament. These stories each contain a central moral or truth that is offered to the late postexilic community. The books of Joel and Song of Songs will also be discussed in this volume. There is certainly much debate about the provenance of these two works, but they will be examined on their own merit with their contributions for all times and places.

Chapter 1

Ezekiel

Congratulations! You have just completed your required education to serve as a classically trained medical doctor. You aced your college requirements, maybe even finishing in three years at the head of your class. Medical schools were lining up to accept you. Through hard work, tears, and sweat you finally completed the rigors of medical school. Your residency was followed by two years of traveling abroad with the Peace Corps as a doctor in a third-world country. The world anxiously awaits the caring practice of your craft. The wife and children who have been so supportive of you during those years of sacrifice also look forward to the benefits that follow such a person of success and influence in the community. Life is good until tragedy strikes. Some young pharmaceutical student invents a series of pills that cure every illness known to humankind. Doctors are now obsolete. All your years of training have proven to be futile. Your hopes, your dreams, your ambitions are now as the dust of the air.

Welcome to the world detailed in the book of Ezekiel. Ezekiel has spent his entire life preparing for the priesthood. His father, his grandfather, his great-grandfather, and so on have all served in the proud lineage of the priests of Israel. But now that rite of passage is gone. Most, if not all, of the leading aristocratic members of Judah's society, including the young eligible priests, have been taken away into captivity in

Babylon. God has shared with Ezekiel that the temple in Jerusalem is about to be destroyed. He finds himself in the middle of a refugee community in a foreign land out of work, surrounded by people who themselves are dazed and confused, and wondering why all this had to happen to his nation or to him personally. This is the world we encounter in the book of Ezekiel.

Ezekiel the Person

The name "Ezekiel" is derived from two Hebrew words—*chazak*, meaning "strength," and *el*, the common Hebrew word for God. Thus, the name Ezekiel can be simply translated as "God strengthens" or "strength of God." When one pronounces this name in Hebrew, the forcefulness of the name itself is clear. It equates to something like "Rock Johnson" in English, a name probably best reserved for a linebacker in the NFL. From our historical perspective the strength inherent in the name Ezekiel provides a foreshadowing for what he must endure throughout his life as the primary prophet of the exile.

Ezekiel 1:3 states that Ezekiel was a priest whose father's name was Buzi. The name "Buzi" implies one who comes from the land or tribe of Buz, sometimes associated with an area in eastern Arabia. Outside of this we know little of Ezekiel's familial background. This verse also calls Ezekiel a priest. Given the time and circumstances, Ezekiel was most likely part of the Zadokite lineage of priests, charged with overseeing the Jerusalem temple, which began in the time of Solomon and was eventually destroyed in 587 BCE at the hands of Nebuchadnezzar and the Babylonians. Ezekiel is a late-coming contemporary of the prophet Jeremiah, who remained in Jerusalem at the outset of the Babylonian captivity. Jeremiah and Ezekiel represent rival sects of the Judean priesthood. Jeremiah, coming from Anathoth, is associated with the lineage of Abiathar, the priest deposed by Solomon for supporting Adonijah's kingship over his own. There is, of course, no specific rivalry addressed in the biblical material between Ezekiel and Jeremiah. Jeremiah offers us a view of the exile from the devastation in Jerusalem and later in Egypt, while Ezekiel reports on life on behalf of the many captives who were taken from their homeland.

Ezekiel was married, according to Ezekiel 24:15-18. A tragic picture unfolds as Ezekiel is instructed not to mourn for his wife, who is about to die, as a picture of strength to the exiles who have also suffered great personal tragedy and loss. His wife is described in beautiful terms: "I am about to take away from you the delight of your eyes" (24:16).

Ezekiel is one of the most eccentric personalities found anywhere in the pages of the Old Testament. His unusual visions, physical manifestations, and strange symbolic acts are unmatched in the Hebrew texts. Other Old Testament figures do unusual things, but Ezekiel's actions approach the bizarre on many levels. A reader only has to look at texts like Ezekiel 4 for classic examples. In this chapter alone, Ezekiel is instructed to play soldier in the sand by building up siege works, laying on his side, and alternating position for a specified period of time and to use human excrement as fuel for baking bread. Ezekiel the priest logs a complaint, stating that he has never defiled himself by eating unclean food. God relents and instructs Ezekiel to use cow excrement instead.

Ezekiel 1:2	5th year	July 593 BCE
Ezekiel 8:1	6th year	September 592 BCE
Ezekiel 20:1	7th year	August 591 BCE
Ezekiel 24:1	9th year	January 588 BCE
Ezekiel 33:21	11th year	January 586 BCE
Ezekiel 40:1	25th year	April 573 BCE

Historical Situation

In Ezekiel 1:2 the author dates the beginning of his book by telling us it is in the fifth year of the exile of King Jehoiachin. King Jehoiachin was taken into captivity, along with the leading elite of Jerusalem, in 598 BCE by Nebuchadnezzar of

Babylon. Nebuchadnezzar allowed Zedekiah to remain on the throne from 598 until the final destruction of Jerusalem and Judah in 587 BCE. Thus, the book of Ezekiel begins somewhere in the vicinity of 593 BCE, five years into the beginning of the Babylonian captivity. Conditions were difficult for those who had been taken into Babylon. The Babylonian army gathered together those taken into exile at staging areas in Israel, then brought them as captives to the land of Babylon. The prophetic ministry of Ezekiel spans the first third of the Babylonian captivity. Ezekiel warns the Israelites that the exile will not be over soon even though, initially, the Jerusalem temple still stood. Some of the Israelites were apparently counting on the prophet Isaiah's words to be correct when he spoke concerning the inviolability of the temple—as long as the temple stood, they would always be protected. In contrast to the common belief, Ezekiel instructs these people to settle in for a lengthy stay. Ezekiel also ministers to his fellow countrymen and women when they learn of the end of Judah and the final destruction of the temple. The latest historical marker found in Ezekiel 29:17 denotes the year 571 BCE. Ezekiel's prophetic tenure was marred by disappointment, hardships, and God's promise of restoration.

Chronology in the Book

Ezekiel is one of only a few books in the Old Testament where a sense of historical dating is important to the author of the book. Ezekiel, Haggai, and Zechariah give the reader a sense of temporal perspective throughout their books. In much of the remaining prophetic materials, however, the reader is only aware of the historical situation within a given book by the book's superscription—an opening title listing kings whose reigns coincided with the ministry of the given prophet (see Isa 1:1; Jer 1:1-3; Amos 1:1). Many of the psalms also have a similar superscription that may be used to suggest a historical context for the psalm.

The book of Ezekiel is replete with many date markers throughout the writing. There are six pivotal dates that serve to provide a chronological framework for the book.

Ezekiel mentions other dates throughout the book, such as the aforementioned Ezekiel 29:17, but the six verses listed above demonstrate the author's desire to communicate to the reader the historical markers as a literary framework for his writing.

Ezekiel 1:1 provides another date of some interest in the book of Ezekiel. The text reads, "In the thirtieth year . . . I saw visions of God." One possible way to interpret the date "thirtieth year" is to apply it to the time that has passed since Ezekiel has begun his prophetic ministry, or 563 BCE. Another possible interpretation is to view this as Ezekiel's age at the beginning of his prophetic ministry. Numbers 4:3 gives this age as the time when a priest becomes eligible to serve in the priestly office. If accurate, this latter interpretation adds a note of mourning present throughout much of the book. At the very time Ezekiel is able to assume his priestly duties, he is whisked away into a foreign land, apart from the priestly heritage and temple.

Unique Features in Ezekiel

Ezekiel stands alone, in many respects, from the collection of Israel's prophetic tradition. First, Ezekiel reads as a collection of first-person reports. The superscription found in Ezekiel 1:2-3, of course, is an early exception as an editorial note. There is much debate among prophetic scholars concerning the authorship and composition of the book of Ezekiel, but the text of Ezekiel contains a collection of first-person accounts of the events of the Babylonian exile, giving us an "insider's view." Unlike most other prophetic texts, which read like a series of thumbnail digital images changing from one scene to the next, Ezekiel is divided into a well-written essay, focusing on three separate themes within the writing: judgment on Judah/Jerusalem (1:1–24:27); oracles against the nations (25:1–32:32); restoration/hope (33–48). The author appears to have written much of the text during the time the activity mentioned in the book takes place. There are some who consider Ezekiel the first actual "writing" prophet among the prophets of Israel. Certainly, other prophets did write and record much of what we have as their message today, but Ezekiel stands alone, as the entire writing of Ezekiel represents this type of written communication. Most of the other prophetic texts appear to be a gathering or piecing together of various messages and stories rather than tightly written essays about contemporary events.

There are also unique literary characteristics found in the book of Ezekiel. The text of Ezekiel is filled with visions (1–3; 8–11; 37; 40–48). Amos, Isaiah, and Jeremiah all recorded visions they had concerning Israel and Judah, but the visions found in Ezekiel are reminiscent of those found in apocalyptic literature. The nature of these visions has often led to fanciful interpretations by ancient and modern interpreters alike. One only has to peruse the local Christian bookstores featuring end-time prophecies to find many creative readings of the book of Ezekiel and Ezekiel's visions.

Along with visions, there are many allegories recorded in the book of Ezekiel. Ezekiel 15:1-8 tells the allegory of the vine, and the allegory of an unfaithful wife occurs in chapter 16. Other allegories used throughout the book of Ezekiel include two eagles (17:1-21); a tall cedar (17:22-24); lion cubs (19:1-9); a smelter (22:17-22); Oholah and Oholibah, two sisters representing Samaria and Jerusalem respectively (23); a boiling pot (24:1-14). In chapter 34 Ezekiel describes God in terms of a good shepherd, reminiscent of Psalm 23.

Another unique literary device in the book of Ezekiel includes the repetition of certain phrases. "You know that I am the LORD" appears sixty-two times. "I, the LORD, have spoken" appears nineteen times. And the phrase Jesus most often used to refer to himself as recorded in the Gospels, "O Mortal" or "Son of Man," appears ninety-three times throughout the book of Ezekiel. Ezekiel makes broad use of symbolic acts throughout the writing. The aforementioned Ezekiel 4 serves as a classic example of the unusual symbolic actions found throughout this book.

The book of Ezekiel breaks tradition with the earlier classical prophets (those who have books bearing their names) and shares much in common with the pre-classical prophets (those who do not have books bearing their names, such as Elijah and Elisha). Ezekiel revives many of the pre-classical traditions that we find in the earlier stories, such as images of God transporting him (3:12; 8:3). We also see this exemplified with the numerous accounts of the elders sitting with him in his home (8:1; 14:1; 20:1). Even the great story of the Valley of Dry Bones in Ezekiel 37 is reminiscent of an age of signs and wonders illuminated in the pages detailing the stories of Elijah and Elisha.

The Texts of Ezekiel

Part 1: Judgment on Jerusalem and Judah, Ezekiel 1:1–24:27

The Superscription, 1:1-3

The historical background for the first section of the book of Ezekiel finds its setting from 593–588 BCE, following the first great deportation of detainees in 598 BCE but before the devastation and destruction of Jerusalem and Judah in 587/586 BCE. Scholars often use the dual date of 587/586 BCE due to Ezekiel 33:21, which records the date of the destruction as the eleventh year, tenth month, according to the Septuagint, or early Greek translation of the Hebrew text. The Masoretic texts (Hebrew Bible), from which we have derived most of our modern English translations, state that the destruction took place in the twelfth year. Working back from the date of 598, when the Babylonians took King Jehoiachin and the first wave of detainees, creates for the careful reader the dilemma of viewing the destruction of Jerusalem in either 587 or 586 BCE.

The book of Ezekiel begins with a lengthy superscription (1:1-3), giving the reader a careful overview of what is to come. Many prophetic books of the Old Testament use this literary device as a way of providing context and background for the prophetic message. For many of these books, it is the only way future generations have for placing the message in a historical and/or geographical context. The Hebrew text reads, "On the fifth day of the fourth month, of my thirtieth year." Although there are different ways to translate this historical marker, I like the thought of Ezekiel turning thirty and facing the daunting reality of being ready to assume his role as a priest, but no longer having access to the Jerusalem temple or the opportunity to serve in this role. The editor, or perhaps the author of this text, also gives a geographical location: the Kebar River. The physical location for the book of Ezekiel is Babylon. The story begins at a tenuous time in a land full of curiosity and danger. In this place we are told that the God of Israel has provided visions for the prophet to see.

Some superscriptions come with biographical information about the prophet, and this is the case with v. 3. We learn that Ezekiel's father, Buzi, was a priest. Many believe that male members of priestly families had little choice but to follow in the family practice of also entering the priesthood. They viewed it as their family's right and tradition. Knowing this bit of information about the prophet Ezekiel is helpful when reading through the message of this prophet.

The Call of Ezekiel, 1:4–3:15

The call of Ezekiel begins with a rather unusual vision. Ezekiel starts having a vision with four strange animals, each having a wheel. Above the animals was a dome, with a sapphire throne above the dome. Ezekiel summarizes this unusual vision by saying that the appearance on the throne was likened to the glory of the Lord (1:28). Out of this strange background a voice speaks to Ezekiel. God's glory is now in Babylon with the first group of exiles and not bound in temporal space to the temple or Jerusalem. This is a profound theological statement for Ezekiel to make. The God of Israel is not bound to time or place. The God of Israel is mobile and not fixed. God may even be found in a "pagan" or "unclean" land such as Babylon. Ezekiel has had the first of what will become many visions. He

Ezekiel

has heard a voice call out from the heavens from a great throne and has fallen to his knees out of a sense of reverence.

God calls Ezekiel for a specific task: to go and speak God's words to the nation of Israel, a nation whose leadership and heart are now in exile in Babylon. In 2:1-2, God calls Ezekiel, to whom God refers as "mortal," to "get up!" The Hebrew phrase transliterated *ben adam* occurs frequently throughout the book of Ezekiel. It is Jesus' favorite term for self-identification, according to the Gospel writers, and the author uses it here to show the difference between the one transmitting the message to Ezekiel, a divine being, and Ezekiel, a mere mortal.

The voice calls for Ezekiel to get up or stand up. Respect and awe are appropriate responses when one encounters a holy being. Moses was instructed to remove his sandals as a sign of reverence when standing before God's presence at the burning bush (Ex 2). But God did not create humanity to be a groveling worm! God created humanity in the very image of God, making humanity not only redeemable but special. Humankind is of noble heritage and birth—not only Israel, but *all* who are created in the image of God. When we focus all of our time on groveling before God and others, we are not ready to accomplish the purposes and tasks for which we were created.

Ezekiel 2:2 records, "A spirit entered into me and set me on my feet." Ezekiel is raised to his feet by the command and authority of the Almighty God. When God calls us to action, God also empowers us for the task at hand. There is a rather mysterious principle about the workings of God. It relates that if we are able to accomplish things on our power or abilities alone, then perhaps we are not fully attaining that which God has in store for us. Can you remember a time when you tried to live the Christian life in your own power or strength? God prepared Ezekiel for a daunting task by lifting him up and establishing a firm message with instructions for Ezekiel to complete.

The call continues as the voice calls Ezekiel to be a prophet to his own people, the Israelites (Ezek 2:3-4). Many prophets—such as Nahum, Jonah, and Obadiah—were called to travel to or to prophesy about other nations. Ezekiel was called by God to be a prophet to his own people. Even as we read these words, we can hear the foreshadowing of the words of Luke's Gospel: "I tell you the truth," he continued, "no prophet is accepted in his own hometown." From the outset, Ezekiel faced a daunting task.

The voice describes the nation of Israel, which in this case refers both to Israel and Judah, even though the Assyrians had previously destroyed Israel over a century earlier. Throughout the books of Hosea and now in Ezekiel, Israel is described as a prostitute who, despite being loved, leaves God's love to chase after false gods as an unfaithful lover chases after new quests. Time after time God has redeemed them, yet Israel spurns God again and again.

God assures Ezekiel that the people will know that a prophet has been with them "whether they hear or fail to hear" (v. 5). Ezekiel's task was not to make the people listen, but simply to be faithful in delivering the message that God placed before him. Ezekiel was not to be the spirit or conscience of the people; he was to share the visions placed before him and allow God to work in the presence and heart of the people. In spite of what several religious leaders have tried over the centuries, you cannot legislate morality or true religion. John Calvin tried to turn Geneva, Switzerland, into a city governed solely by biblical law. As history records, Calvin was directly involved in the burning of Michael Servetus because he dared to defy the church law established by Calvin and his followers. The Spanish Inquisition, a dark chapter of the Roman Catholic Church, also reminds us that when we try to manipulate or control the lives of others, we are in danger of creating tyranny, fear, and evil in the lives of others. In our attempt to save or convert others, we can easily become a source of evil ourselves. When God gives us a message today to deliver, we are responsible as a messenger for delivering that message. By God's grace we deliver that message with love, humility, and with all the courage that God's spirit can place within us. The results of that message, however, are the purview of God. God called Ezekiel to let those around him know that a prophet was in their midst. God had not forgotten them even though they now found themselves in exile in a strange and foreign land.

The voice further instructs Ezekiel not to be afraid, even though the dangers are real. It is not paranoia when someone is really out to get you. Verse 6 describes the dangers as "though briers and thorns are all around you and you live among scorpions." Ezekiel faced real dangers. He faced a political reality of living as a captive in a foreign land. There are dangers in our world today as well. People often become agitated and angry with those who speak for God. At times people become angry when one shares the good news of Jesus Christ with them. People who are caught up in the grips of a sinful lifestyle don't always react well to those who show them that there is futility on their current path. Genuine Christianity will be persecuted, not all the time and not every day, but along the way you will be persecuted for being "different," being a "do-gooder," or sometimes you may even be called "holier than thou."

In these times of danger, do not be afraid. God is there. Even in foreign places and lands, God is there looking after us, going before us, protecting us as we seek to do what God has called us to do. Jeremiah 1:17-19 states that Jeremiah, like Ezekiel, was instructed to face opposition. God's people are called to overcome our fears. Whatever those dangers may be, whether external or internal, we must face our fears and willingly complete the tasks that God has set before us.

In Ezekiel 2:9–3:2 God instructs Ezekiel to take a scroll that is set before him and to eat it. Verse 10 describes the scroll: "Written on it were words of lamentation and mourning and woe." Ezekiel is obedient to what God has instructed him to do. He is to bring a message of devastation for Jerusalem. He adds that Judah is finished as a nation. Apparently many of the exiles believed they would be going back to their homeland of Judah very soon because the temple still stood in Judah, erroneously believing God would deliver them for the sake of God's temple. Ezekiel instructs them to settle down, pack a lunch, and prepare to be in exile for a long while. The truth is that we don't get to choose our circumstances in life. We don't pick our parents. We don't pick our nationality of birth. Often we may feel like Frodo in *Lord of the Rings*. We didn't ask to be the bearer of the ring! But the call of Ezekiel reminds us that the call to service is the call to accept all that it entails, even when it means delivering a message that we know will not be received well.

God has prepared Ezekiel for this task. Ezekiel 3:8-9 reminds us once again about the foreshadowing of Ezekiel's purposes inherent in his very name: "I have made your face hard against their faces, and your forehead hard against their foreheads. Like the hardest stone, harder than flint, I have made your forehead; do not fear them or be dismayed at their looks, for they are a rebellious house." Remember the name Ezekiel in Hebrew? *Chazak El*—God strengthens!

A long time ago, the spirit of God came to me and said, "Go speak my words." My whole life wasn't laid out before me. I had no idea where or how this request was going to play out, but I am so glad I said yes to that request early in my adult journey. I still have much work to do in this life as I try to be more faithful as a disciple each day. Some days I do pretty well. Others I fall flat on my face. I challenge you as a reader of these words if there is something that God has placed before you today to do, please do not put it off any longer. If God is calling you to "go speak these words," then get up out of your seat and be the person that God is calling you to be! I promise you that, like Ezekiel, your life will never be the same again, and you will never regret answering that call.

Destruction Is Coming to Jerusalem and Judah, 4:1–24:27

Ezekiel 4–24 records the first of three main emphases Ezekiel is passing along to those who are with him in captivity in Babylon. This first series of messages includes words of warning to the people who are clinging to the hope of a quick return to quit looking for false hope. It is sometime between 593 and 587 BCE. The exiles were clinging to a hope offered by Isaiah in the eighth century BCE, described by Old Testament scholars as

Ezekiel

"the inviolability of Jerusalem." This belief maintained that as long as the temple and Jerusalem stood, there was still hope for them. Ezekiel tells the people to prepare for a long stay in Babylon. Ezekiel, like Jeremiah, warns the people to not place their trust in brick and mortar, but in the God of their forefathers. Judgment has come because they have been a disobedient people.

In Ezekiel 4, Ezekiel uses three separate symbolic acts to communicate his message of the coming destruction for Jerusalem. In vv. 1-3 Ezekiel is instructed to re-create a picture of the siege of Jerusalem. The ancient tactic of besiegement is a basic tactic of warfare. The cities are surrounded by the attacking armies. Sources of food and water are cut off from those inside the cities. The attacking armies simply waited for the people to starve and become unable to offer a reasonable defense. Then they would attack and storm the city. Many times cities in ancient times were taken without much of a struggle because of their weakened condition.

As a youngster I once had a sandbox that was about three feet wide and six feet in length. I loved to make two walls opposing each other, then to set toy soldiers in key positions along and behind the walls. I would then try to knock down the soldiers from the opposite side of the walls with rocks or sometimes firecrackers. I called it "playing soldier." In the winter months, when it was too cold outside to play, I would lay a blanket down on the floor with strategic wrinkles in place and set my soldiers along the various crinkles and folds. One day my father watched me playing and asked me what I was doing. I told him I was playing "commandos." It was the height of the Vietnam War, and I read the newspaper even in the first grade, thanks to a mother who read to me constantly. I would also watch the evening news with my parents, so I heard the word "commandos" many times during those years. He simply laughed and asked me if I had any idea what the word meant. Of course I really didn't, but it sure sounded like a good word to use when I was "playing soldier."

In one sense Ezekiel is "playing soldier" in the sand. In another sense he is drawing a poignant picture that Jerusalem is about to be invaded and destroyed. Have you ever needed someone to draw you a picture before you could understand what message the person was intending to transmit? Ezekiel is instructed to make this message crystal clear: War is coming to Jerusalem.

Verse 3 records a scene that is troubling to those who profess the Christian faith. Ezekiel is instructed to place an iron plate between himself and the siege works he has constructed. This symbolically represents God's relationship to the residents of Judah and Jerusalem. God will not be there to help them against the armies of Babylon. They are on their own. Jerusalem, the temple, and the nation of Judah are about to suffer brutally at the hands of the Babylonians. God's salvation will be sadly absent from this fateful day.

The second symbolic act God instructs Ezekiel to perform is detailed in vv. 4-8. Ezekiel is instructed to lie on his side as a warning to the people concerning the length of their captivity. Ezekiel is instructed to lie on his left side for 390 days for the sins of Israel, the former northern nation that was destroyed by the Assyrian Empire in 722 BCE. He was then to lie on his right side for forty days as a representation of the sins of Judah, the southern kingdom. The Septuagint reads 190 days rather than 390 days for the length of the punishment for the people. The number 190 actually comes closer to the end of the captivity that took place in 539 BCE (thus, 532 BCE is the resulting date when taking 190 from the date of 722 BCE rather than 232 BCE when taking 390 from the date of 722 BCE).

Can you imagine if your minister came to your next Sunday morning worship service bound in ropes and simply laid on his or her left side as the Sunday sermon? That is precisely what Ezekiel said he did as a symbolic act for fourteen months. In vv. 7-8 Ezekiel is instructed to turn his face toward the coming siege of Jerusalem. Judgment is coming!

The third and final symbolic act found in Ezekiel 4 is found in the instruction God gives to Ezekiel concerning the preparation of bread. The voice instructs Ezekiel to make bread for himself using human excrement for fuel. Allowances for the removal of human waste are found in Deuteronomy 23:12-14. In v. 14 Ezekiel responds to the words with protest. He is a priest and has never eaten food that is considered unclean before. God relents and instructs Ezekiel to use cow excrement instead. The remaining verses of Ezekiel 4 give further explanation for this most unusual request. It is yet another symbol of the atrocities the people of Jerusalem are about to suffer at the hand of the Babylonians. The book of Lamentations offers in poetic form insights into the horrible realities suffered by the inhabitants of Jerusalem during the siege of Babylon from 588 to 587/586 BCE. For a brief reminder please refer to Lamentations 4:1-11, which details the severity of the siege with women boiling their own children in order to have food to eat.

One may ask how these symbolic acts describing the coming destruction of Jerusalem can possibly relate to our contemporary world. Let me briefly make three possible suggestions. First, this text reminds the reader that God's judgments are real. We enjoy all that we enjoy today only by the grace of God. The people of Jerusalem had turned their faces away from the God of their ancestry. Life is so fragile. We are to live in gratitude for the grace God affords us each day. Second, God can see you through any difficulty. These words were also filled with meaning for those who had already experienced the atrocities of being ripped from their homes and families. God has not forgotten them even in a foreign and unclean land. In fact, the hope of Israel lay not in those in Jerusalem, but rather in those who were struggling with Ezekiel in Babylon. Third, these texts remind many of us of just how blessed we are in our worlds of suburbia today. We drive nice cars, to our nice jobs, and return to our comfortable homes without a thought that life could be so different. Unfortunately, too many in our global village do not have nice cars, jobs, or comfortable homes awaiting them each day. For those of us who have been so blessed, we are to use these blessings not for ourselves, but to seek the well-being of others around us. Whether that be a homeless person in a downtown area or a small child in Haiti wondering where their next meal will come from, we are called to be God's presence in a broken world.

The symbolic acts continue in Ezekiel 5. Ezekiel shaves his head and beard, dividing the hair into thirds. He burns one-third on his battlefield. One-third is cut to pieces with a sword. One-third is scattered with the wind. These acts once again point to the coming destruction of Jerusalem. One-third of the people will die during the siege of the city, one-third will be killed in armed conflict, and one-third will be spread about randomly as refugees. Ezekiel is instructed to tie a few of his hairs into the thread of his robe in v. 3. This last bit of hair represents the remnant that will be kept safe during the destruction of Jerusalem.

Ezekiel 6 and 7 detail Ezekiel speaking out publicly about idolatry, pronouncing judgment on the land of Judah. In 8–11, Ezekiel sees a vision focusing on the Jerusalem temple. In chapters 10 and 11 the glory of the Lord departs from the temple and Jerusalem. In chapters 15 through 18 one finds a series of allegories, all pointing to the destruction that is coming.

Why all this doom and gloom? Ezekiel chronicles the reasons for this destruction in Ezekiel 22, listing several sins of Israel. Israel is guilty of not keeping the covenant (5:6), violence (11:6), listening to false prophets (13:1-16), engaging mediums (13:17-23), corruption and injustice (22:7, 12), adultery, and defaming that which is to be holy (22:26). Yet with all this emphasis on judgment, there is still a tenor of hope sprinkled throughout the words of Ezekiel once the judgment is past. Ezekiel paints a picture of hope for the people of Israel through those remaining in captivity (11:14-21). He describes a coming exodus from Babylon in 20:33-44, where once again God will winnow those guilty of transgressions during the exile from those who are faithful. This second winnowing will occur during their return trip to the land of promise.

The conclusion of the first part of Ezekiel contains one of the saddest stories recorded in the Old Testament. In Ezekiel 24:1-2, Ezekiel receives a message stating that the siege of

Ezekiel

Jerusalem has come to pass. Ezekiel responds with an allegory of a boiling pot in 24:3-14. Then, the unthinkable happens. God shares with Ezekiel that God is about to take Ezekiel's "dearest treasure." Furthermore, God instructs Ezekiel not to mourn or to enter into the normal pattern of remembering a loved one who has passed. God shares this message with the people, and the next morning Ezekiel's wife is dead. This has always appeared to me to be one of the coldest and most hollow pictures of God's working anywhere in the Old Testament. It is not enough to be taken from your homeland into a strange and foreign land, but now Ezekiel must face that which is to come with uncertainty, alone, without a companion to aid him. To make matters worse, God instructs Ezekiel not to mourn, and if he sighs, to do so quietly. Wow. These are heavy words indeed. Now, God is using Ezekiel's life and family in order to convey a message to those who are in captivity. Ezekiel's wife represents the heaviness the people are about to endure with the cataclysmic loss of Jerusalem and the temple. The normal ritual of mourning is frivolous, mattering very little. Following the tragic loss of his wife, God tells Ezekiel to be silent until the news arrives in Babylon of the final end of Judah (24:25-27). God has a new message for Ezekiel, v. 27a records: "On that day your mouth shall be opened to the one who has escaped, and you shall speak and no longer be silent." This terrible passage ends with a spark of hope. God has a new message of restoration and hope. Even when the day is darkest, there is always hope with God.

These sad words are reminiscent of a poem by Robert Browning, "Measuring Life":

> Measure thy life by loss instead of gain,
> Not by the wine drunk, but the wine poured forth;
> For love's strength standeth in love's sacrifice,
> And whoso suffers most hath most to give.
> For labor, the common lot of man,
> Is part of the kind Creator's plan;
> And he is king whose brow is wet
> With the pearl-gemmed crown of honest sweat,

> Some glorious day, this understood,
> All toilers will be a brotherhood,
> With brain or hand the purpose is one,
> And the Master-workman, God's own Son.[1]

Part 2: Oracles Against the Nations, 25:1–32:32

Ezekiel receives his instruction to be silent in January 588 BCE. During the two years that follow, Jerusalem endures a terrible time of siege and devastation. As instructed, Ezekiel is silent during this two-year period. Commentators often refer to this section of Ezekiel as the "silent phase."

The material found in these chapters contains messages of judgment against the nations that surround the ancient homelands of Israel and Judah. God speaking through Ezekiel offers pronouncements against Ammon, Moab, Edom, Philistia, Tyre, and Egypt. There are many superscriptions throughout this body of writing, dating this portion of Ezekiel to the two-year intervening period between the first and last section of the book. It is also curious that the author/editor of these superscriptions does not place them in chronological order. The author/editor of this material seemingly is more concerned with content and genre rather than portraying a historical timeline or historical narrative. These oracles against the nations are common in the prophetic writings of ancient Israel. Amos 1–2 records a lengthy roll call of sins the nations surrounding Israel were guilty of committing. Isaiah and Jeremiah also include lengthy passages of oracles against the nations. The primary message of these judgments on the foreign nations is that the Babylonians will overcome and destroy each of these nations before the restoration of Israel will begin (28:24-26).

Part 3: Restoration and Hope, 33:1–48:35

A common theme runs throughout the texts of much of the prophetic material. Judgment is almost always followed with tender mercy. Growing up in northern Ohio, I remember well those times of discipline by my father. He was a native of Oklahoma and always wore a wide cowboy belt. That belt and I were not friends. My father led the music in church while my mother was the church pianist. Like others before me, I really believed that the morning worship service consisted of having a prayer, singing a hymn, and taking Wayne outside to spank him! But I also remember those times of discipline were usually followed by a trip to the ice cream shop right around the corner from our modest home. In our home, mercy almost always followed judgment.

In Ezekiel 33–48 there has been a transformation in the message and person of Ezekiel. The reader is moved from the corporate responsibility of a nation to the individual responsibility as a person. This is something new in Old Testament theology. God now gives Ezekiel a pastoral charge: to bring the people back to obedience to the covenant that was broken time and again throughout the histories of Israel and Judah. One could rightly argue that Ezekiel's new role is to bring consolation to the people. Like the latter half of Isaiah, he is to bring comfort and hope to those who are languishing in captivity.

You Are a Watchperson, 33:1-20

Ezekiel's new role is exemplified in the first message that God passes along to Ezekiel in 33:1-20. Ezekiel is told in verse 7, "So you, mortal, I have made a sentinel for the house of Israel; whenever you hear a word from my mouth, you shall give them warning from me." God gives Ezekiel a special charge. Leaders are accountable for their action of leadership. Ezekiel calls the prophetic office a sentry or watchperson accountable for the care of the people of Israel. The leader is responsible to speak the truth in a compelling and responsible manner. Verse 8 states that we are accountable for giving words of warning to others who are in harm's way. Once the warning is given, our task is complete. We are not responsible for what others do with that warning, but we are charged with calling out with a clarion call the danger that others may face. Verse 9 reinforces the accountability of the individual. If the warning is given, the individual is not responsible for what transpires to them, but if the warning is not given, the watchman is responsible for the outcome. It is never easy to sit back and watch friends and family member self-destruct. It is painful and almost unbearable. It hurts us to watch our loved ones dangling closer and closer to the precipice, knowing that any moment unwanted or unintended consequences may result.

Why are people not listening to the message that is being proclaimed by God's watchpersons today? Faithful men and women are proclaiming the truths of God and doing their best to live a lifestyle consistent with these truths, yet it appears that this message is losing ground each day in our culture. Scandal after scandal has eroded our trust and appreciation for men and women that God has placed as watchpersons over us. The corruption of so many of our religious leaders that became public media fodder beginning in the 1980s, the actions of cultic groups in Waco and Jonestown, and the betrayal of sacred trusts exemplified by so many religious leaders toward children have all added to the general mistrust of religious leaders. There is without a doubt a crisis of trust. A world that knows not the favor of a loving God looks to us and simply says, "Why should I listen to you?"

Ezekiel 33:10-20 moves the focus away from the watchman to the responsibility of the individual, culminating in the question in v. 10b: "How then can we live?" In v. 11 the answer is made clear: "Turn back, turn back from your evil ways." God's grace is not limited to the pages of the New Testament. Throughout the entirety of the Old and New Testaments, we see the repeated theme that God desires mercy over judgment. But there is a consistent catch. We are to follow the ways of God and acknowledge God. The people are encouraged that if they will simply turn back their hearts to the God of their forefathers and do that which is right, they will be spared (vv. 14-16).

This famous passage found in Ezekiel 33 offers three important issues for us to consider today. First, if you have been entrusted with a position of leadership, then by all means take that position seriously. You are responsible before God for the way you lead others. You are a watchperson. Second, we are all responsible individually before God. Flip Wilson became famous for saying "the devil made me do it." When we turn our backs to the ways and will of God, we are ultimately responsible, not those who are tempting us. Third, this passage is a call to those who find themselves in places of exile to finish strong the race set before them. Don't give up, because God does not give up on us. To a remnant of hurting refugees, Ezekiel is urging steadfastness.

Messages of Hope, 33:21–39:29

With Ezekiel's new role comes a new message. Gone are the messages of judgment and destruction, replaced with the message of hope for a brighter day ahead. This message is consistent with other apocalyptic literature throughout the Bible. It is the giving of hope to those readers and listeners that life will get better. Maybe not today, maybe not tomorrow, but one day there will be a time of restoration. Ezekiel 34:11-25 provides a beautiful image of the God of Israel as a good shepherd, reminiscent of Psalm 23 and anticipating the words of Jesus as recorded in Matthew 25. Ezekiel anticipates the nation of Israel once again being ruled by a Davidic king as a sign of the restoration (34:23-24). Two important visions found in the last section of Ezekiel dominate this message of hope: the valley of dry bones (37:1-14) and the new temple and nation (40–48).

The Valley of Dry Bones, 37:1-14

Most of us are familiar with the popular nursery rhyme "Humpty Dumpty."

> Humpty Dumpty sat on the wall.
>   Humpty Dumpty had a great fall.
> All the King's horses and all the King's men
>   Couldn't put Humpty Dumpty together again.

This popular nursery rhyme speaks of the human condition, reminding us that many things cannot simply be rebuilt and that some things cannot be replaced. If we are not careful, this can lead us into a path of fatalism, which states that nothing we do really matters because our lives or situations simply cannot be helped, that we have no control over what happens. Or we can be drawn into the belief that everything is already predestined so that we once again have no control over anything and simply must accept whatever fate befalls us. The vision of Ezekiel 37 refutes both of these erroneous positions. The God of Abraham, Isaac, Jacob, and the exile is able to bring about the impossible from the possible. This vision screams that all things are possible with God.

The God of Israel can restore life to any situation. The vision recorded in Ezekiel 37:1-14 is another instance of Ezekiel having more in common with the pre-classical prophets than the classical prophets. Here, Ezekiel seemingly is transported to a valley where a major catastrophe has taken place, probably a great battle. The landscape is strewn with corpses and decaying bodies. As a priest Ezekiel was not to come near a corpse except for the body of an immediate family member (Num 19:16-18). Verse 2 records that the bones were dry and calcified. All hope for restoration or resuscitation was gone for these bodies. This valley represented a place without hope. This must have been akin to the feelings of many members of the exilic community in Babylon. Jerusalem was gone. The temple was destroyed. Loved ones were scattered, and many of them must have been presumed dead. The foreign king ruling over them was also constantly imposing the worship of the native gods of Babylon, calling upon the people of Judah to abandon their God and to abandon hope.

God asks Ezekiel a question in v. 3: "Mortal, can these bones live?" Ezekiel wisely allows God to propose an answer to that question: "You know." Ezekiel recognizes the power of God to accomplish seemingly impossible tasks. Some in our world deny the existence of God and especially God's ability to possess power or have any effect on the "real" world. More than likely there were many in Babylon who were among the exiles who felt the same way. Where was God when all this happened to us? Where was God when Jerusalem was destroyed? Why would a powerful God allow God's own temple to be destroyed?

God further instructs Ezekiel to prophesy or preach to these dried-up bones. God works together with Ezekiel in bringing about this symbolic act or vision. Humanity's place in the workings of God should never be overlooked or underestimated. In v. 7 Ezekiel prophesies to the bones. As he speaks, the bones begin to rattle and come together throughout the valley. This is not your garden-variety vision! Once again, the *ruach* of God plays an important part in the work of re-creation. *Ruach* is the Hebrew word for "spirit" or "breath," used repeatedly in the Old Testament and playing a prominent act in the story of creation in Genesis 2. This breath, spirit, or wind rejuvenated this mighty army of bones, and they were filled with life once again. Can you imagine Ezekiel's response?

Verse 12 holds the key to properly understanding this dramatic vision: "I am going to open your graves, and bring you up from your graves, O my people; and I will bring you back to the land of Israel." Those with Ezekiel who were part of the Babylonian exile were beginning to lose all hope and belief in the power and divine grace of the Almighty God. The God of Israel will once again bring the nation of Israel back to life. The dry bones represent a nation who lived in exile for a lengthy time—make no mistake, they were dead and gone! The bones represent the hope that had perished. The bones were also separated. They had to come back together to be made whole. A God who can restore life to dry bones can surely gather people from the disparate nations where they were scattered and restore them to their promised land. Ezekiel calls the people to believe that this is not the end. God is not finished with them yet, and they will have a bright future once more.

Many in our world, even believers, have given up on God. This can occur when we see too many Christians behaving badly or selfishly. It can occur when we see the wicked prospering while good, decent people continue to struggle. But these thoughts are wrongheaded! Ezekiel 37 reminds us that there is always hope with God. God can restore God's people. God can mend the brokenhearted and the bleeding heart. God can even turn that callous, bitter soul into a joyous, happy spirit.

> All the King's horses and all the King's men
> Couldn't put Humpty together again.

But God can!

Ezekiel 37:15-28 is the forgotten portion of this chapter, but it is vital to the message of Ezekiel. God instructs Ezekiel to fetch two sticks and to write the name of Judah on one and Israel on the other. God commands Ezekiel to place them together as a sign that Israel and Judah will be reunited once again under a Davidic king who will lead them to greatness once again. The purpose for this reunion is summarized in verse 28: "Then the nations shall know that I the LORD sanctify Israel, when my sanctuary is among them forevermore."

Ezekiel 38 and 39 are two of the most abused and misunderstood chapters in the Old Testament. Many persons who specialize in end-time prophecy love to lift these two chapters out of their original context, place them alongside other similar-sounding texts, and build all kinds of fanciful interpretations for anticipating the end of days. These are two important texts in Ezekiel, but only when placed in their proper context as examples of further visions given to Ezekiel of restoration and hope—hope that comes to a fulfillment in approximately 539 BCE when the exilic community of Israel is allowed to return to their homeland in Judah. These two chapters extol God reaffirming Ezekiel that when they are restored once again, nations will take notice and try to assert themselves preeminently upon them, but Israel should not be afraid because God is not going to step aside this time as when God allowed the Babylonians to destroy Jerusalem.

The New Temple and New Nation, 40–48

Ezekiel 40–48 is the climax of the visions of Ezekiel. This grand extended vision promises a new day with a new temple and a renewed nation of Israel living back in the land of promise. Ezekiel 40–42 gives intricate detail into the size and dimensions of the new temple. This vision is a symbol of the hope for a brighter day for those who are suffering in Babylon. It is reminiscent for a Christian audience today of the concluding words of the New Testament apocalyptic work at the end of Revelation. Revelation 21 gives specific details of a new Jerusalem as a symbol of hope for those losing their lives during intense Roman persecution. They, too, looked forward to a brighter day when they could enjoy freedom from persecution once again. This was especially true for the author of the text, who claims to be exiled himself on the isle of Patmos. Perhaps the most striking feature of Ezekiel is found in Ezekiel 43:1-12. Here one finds the restoration of the glory of the Lord, once again located within the new temple. Restoration will be made complete.

Conclusion

Ezekiel is a wonderful book that is often set aside because we fear our own inadequacy in interpreting the apocalyptic language contained within its pages. When one ventures into this text, the reader is richly rewarded, beginning with a frightful message of judgment and doubt but ultimately concluding with a message of hope and restoration. There are life lessons throughout this mysterious book of antiquity. Ezekiel reminds us that life can be hard and oppressive, but there is always hope when one has faith in a living God.

For Further Reading

Ackroyd, Peter R. *Exile and Restoration.* The Old Testament Library. Philadelphia: Westminster Press, 1968.

Bunn, John T. "Ezekiel." *The Broadman Bible Commentary*, vol. 6. Nashville: Broadman Press, 1971.

Crenshaw, James L. *Old Testament Story and Faith: A Literary and Theological Approach*. Peabody MA: Hendrickson Publishers, 1986.

Driver, S. R. *An Introduction to the Literature of the Old Testament*. New York: Meridian Books, 1960.

Eichrodt, Walther. *Ezekiel*. The Old Testament Library. Philadelphia: Westminster Press, 1970.

Laffey, Alice L. *An Introduction to the Old Testament: A Feminist Perspective*. Philadelphia: Fortress Press, 1988.

O'Dell, Margaret S. *Ezekiel*. Smyth & Helwys Bible Commentary. Macon GA: Smyth & Helwys, 2005.

Rendtorff, Rolf. *The Old Testament: An Introduction*. Philadelphia: Fortress Press, 1986.

West, James King. *Introduction to the Old Testament*. New York: Macmillan Publishing Company, 1981.

Wright, Christopher J. H. *The Message of Ezekiel*. The Bible Speaks Today. Leicester, England: InterVarsity Press, 2001.

Note

[1] Robert Browning, "Measuring Life," in *Poems for Daily Needs*, ed. Thomas Curtis Clark (New York: Round Table Press, Inc., 1936) 179.

Chapter 2

Isaiah

"Comfort, O comfort my people, says your God. Speak tenderly to Jerusalem, and cry to her that she has served her term, that her penalty is paid, that she has received from the LORD's hand double for all her sins."—Isaiah 40:1-2

These words of comfort and hope are the beginning of the call of another prophet in the latter part of Isaiah. The call received by this prophet is radically different from the words found in Isaiah 1–39. The reader is now propelled a century and a half into the future from the end of the eighth century into the middle of the sixth century. The writer has been called to offer words of hope and encouragement to an embattled people, who have suffered greatly at the hands of the Babylonians. The words of Ezekiel must have seemed like a distant memory. Ezekiel had instructed the exiles in Babylon to settle in, but surely the words he spoke about a new day must be near! Into this world comes another prophet, anonymously offering hope and comfort to a desperate people.

Isaiah 40–66 has been the source of much controversy, discussion, and theological tension throughout the last century. The differences between Isaiah 40–66 and Isaiah 1–39 are marked and undeniable. The writer, or writers, responsible for these twenty-seven chapters remains hidden behind the words of the text. We know absolutely nothing about this "prophet," except that the writer is the closest contact we have with the events of the latter part of the Babylonian captivity and the early days of the postexilic community in Palestine. Isaiah 40–66 is often titled the "Book of Consolation." John R. Sampey referred to these words as the "heart of the Old Testament."[1] Dr. Samuel Tang, one of my Old Testament professors during my seminary education, shared with his students that remembering the divisions in Isaiah was fairly easy. Just remember the number of chapters in the Bible, sixty-six, with thirty-nine chapters in the Old Testament and twenty-seven in the New Testament. Likewise, Isaiah has thirty-nine chapters associated with the eighth century, describing the ministry of Isaiah of Jerusalem. Isaiah 40–66, which is twenty-seven chapters, brings words of hope and restoration during the middle to late sixth century.

Understanding the Divisions in Isaiah

Honest discussion concerning the different divisions in the book of Isaiah has become a shibboleth for many who relate to evangelical churches in the United States today. This minefield ranks second only to the theological hotbed associated with one's interpretation of Genesis 1–11. Contributing largely to this problem is the manner in which most modern readers approach Scripture in general. It is fair to assume that most modern readers rarely read more than a few verses of any given text at a time. We have been so programmed into a Sunday school or Bible study reading that we simply focus on a few verses or, at most, a chapter at a time. When one reads only a few verses at a time in Isaiah, one can easily miss the dramatic shift that takes place between Isaiah 39 and Isaiah 40. When one reads the text of Isaiah as a whole, however, one readily acknowledges at least two, if not three, major time periods represented in this work. Some readers want to maintain that the God referred to in Scripture is wholly capable of providing the eighth-century prophet information of what is yet to come two centuries later. Assuming for a moment that this understanding of God is correct, there is still much evidence that suggests multiple authors for this prophetic writing.

Here are a few of the reasons why scholars suggest that the author of Isaiah 40–66 cannot be the Isaiah of the eighth century, associated with Isaiah 1–39. The historical events mentioned in the texts relate two separate time periods. Isaiah 1–39 repeatedly refers to an Isaiah who is a temple prophet, associated with the royalty of Judah, and who issues a prophetic word about both Israel to the north and Judah to the south (6:1; 10:5). The author of Isaiah 40–66 describes events taking place in the sixth century among the exiles in Babylon (43:14; 44:28; 45:1) and later in the postexilic community back in Jerusalem (64:10-11). The theological view of the God of Israel is different. Isaiah 1–39 views the God of Israel as transcendent and distant while Isaiah 40–66 views God as near to those in exile. Isaiah 1–39 is filled with judgment and rebuke while the second half of Isaiah is filled with words of comfort and hope. The name "Isaiah" itself is never mentioned in Isaiah 40–66, and there is a major shift in language and literary style in the Hebrew text between Isaiah 1–39 and 40–66.

But the question must be raised: Why would a later writer append his own words to a text that describes the events that transpired a century and a half earlier? There are many plausible solutions to this question. One such answer is that the book itself as a whole was not completed until at least the time of the postexilic community and that the earlier tradition of the eighth-century prophet Isaiah was combined with a story that took place in the exile and beyond. If Isaiah 1–39 was in written form prior to the exile, then it is possible that members of an Isaiah school of prophets were continuing on in the tradition of Isaiah and felt authorized to include their own story to this earlier text. Isaiah 8:16-18 gives evidence of such an Isaiah school, or prophetic disciples in the tradition of Isaiah.

Historical Situation

Unfortunately, we know so very little about the author of the latter part of Isaiah. There is no superscription, no biographical detail about the author's background, and no extra biblical account identifying who this writer/prophet may be. Isaiah 40:1-11 is often described as the call of Second Isaiah, instructing this prophet to care for the people in captivity in Babylon during the latter part of the Babylonian captivity, 587/586 to 539 BCE. Since there are no allusions to Ezekiel or his message in these words, we may assume that the words of Isaiah 40–66 relate to the middle and last third of the Babylonian captivity. There is expectation that Cyrus, the Persian king, identified as the anointed one or messiah in Isaiah 44:28 and 45:1, will be the great hero of the exiles, defeating Babylon and allowing this community to return to their native land. Though still in captivity, there is expectation and a glimmer of hope glistening through the words of this later Isaiah. In Isaiah 55–66 the author is now apparently back in the land of promise, walking in the midst of the devastation. The return is now complete, but larger questions loom: What next? How do the returnees worship without the temple? Though the exile has ended, now the task of rebuilding and reconstructing lives and meaning occupies the remaining words of Isaiah.

The Texts of Isaiah 40–66

Part 1: The Prophet of Hope in the Exile, 40-55

The Call of the Prophet of Hope, 40:1-11

The first words of Isaiah 40 summarize the message of this prophet of hope in the exile. He has come to bring hope to a people who have little good news. The time of the end of the exile is drawing near. The call of the prophet of the exile is a call to prepare the way for the working of God in bringing about the end of the Babylonian Empire and the restoration of the exilic community back to their homeland. Verse 3 should be familiar with readers of the New Testament as it is quoted in Matthew 3:3, Mark 1:3, and Luke 3:4 in reference to John the Baptist preparing the way for the coming of the Messiah. As Jesus of Nazareth brought good news to the world through his life, death, and resurrection, so too the prophet of the exile brings good news, or salvation, to a people literally enslaved by a conquering nation. Through a Christological reading, the prophet of the exile becomes John the Baptist, making way for the work that God is bringing to the exiled community. Like Ezekiel 34 and Psalm 23, the God of Israel is likened once again to a good shepherd in Isaiah 40:11: "He will feed his flock like a shepherd; he will gather the lambs in his arms, and carry them in his bosom, and gently lead the mother sheep." From the outset and throughout Isaiah 40–55, the God of Israel is portrayed in terms of endearment. Gone are the words of rebuke and judgment so prominent in Isaiah 1–39.

Perseverance in Times of Trouble, 40:27-31

The prophet of hope in the exile responds with a beautiful hymn in Isaiah 40:27-31. Claus Westermann surmises the author of this poem is responding to a community lament, reminiscent in the words of v. 27: "My way is hidden from the LORD, and my right is disregarded by my God." The exiles in Babylon had grown despondent, thinking that all hope is gone. They were asking the question asked by so many in our postmodern world today: Where is God? How can we continue to give credence to the concept of a just and holy God, who is described as light and love, in a world that is filled with so much darkness? This same question is asked many times in the psalms (see Pss 37 and 73). The "hiddenness" of God is a common theme throughout the psalms and in other hymns throughout the Old Testament.

    The author of Isaiah 40:28-31 responds to this question about the absence of God with a dramatic statement of trust and faith. The God of creation does not grow weary or tired as we understand such states of being. God grants strength to the weary and engages the weak with power. Westermann calls this a great paradox. God brings down the strong, the noble, the proud, but lifts up the weary, the weak, and the downtrodden.[2] These words remind us of what Jim Collins describes as the Stockdale Paradox. Collins describes the Stockdale Paradox as accepting the brutal facts of reality while at the same time never doubting the eventual success of the endgame. The Stockdale Paradox is named after Admiral Jim Stockdale, who was the ranking officer of the "Hanoi Hilton" prisoner war camp during the Vietnam War. From 1965 to 1973 Stockdale was personally tortured over twenty times. Stockdale related to Collins some of his experiences in a personal interview. Stockdale shared that those who didn't make it out of the POW camps in Vietnam were the optimists. Stockdale explained, "The optimists, oh, they were the ones who said, 'We're going to be out by Christmas.' And Christmas would come, and Christmas would go. Then they'd say, 'We're going to be out by Easter.' And Easter would come, and Easter would go. And then Thanksgiving, and then it would be Christmas again. And they died of a broken heart."[3] Surely there were many optimists who were taken into exile who were now dead and gone. The prophet of hope in the exile brings words of courage and strength to those who are ready to quit or give up, waiting upon the God of their forefathers for deliverance.

    Verse 31 is one of my favorite verses in all of God's Word. When I was able to run long distances, I would often sing this verse in my mind over and over again during a difficult stretch. Those who do not give up on God will be rewarded with the exchange of strength in the place of weakness. The Hebrew word for hope is the same root word used also for a rope or a spider's web. The Hebrew word calls to mind an exchange. God can empower us and exchange our weakness for God's strength. How many times have we heard the modern saying "When you are at the end of your rope, tie a knot and hang on!" In one sense, that is what this prophet of hope is offering to the people, but with a promise in exchange for their doubt. This verse is also a beautiful representation of the spiritual journey. Some days we are soaring on the wings of eagles. On rare occasions we are able to enjoy those mountaintop experiences. We are flying high at these times. On other days we are running the race that is set before us, day after day accomplishing the tasks to which we have been called. But in the overall scheme of life, most of our days are not spent flying or running; most of our days we find ourselves in the persistent slow walk of making it through the mundane, day-to-day activities. This verse reminds us that in all stages and places of life, God is there, giving us the strength to live each day in a manner worthy of the name of Christ.

The Suffering Servant: Poem 1, 42:1-4

In 1892 Bernhard Duhm published a commentary on Isaiah. In his commentary Duhm isolated four poems and designated them as Suffering Servant poems (42:1-4; 49:1-6; 50:4-9; 52:13–53:12). Duhm contended that these poems were written by an author other than the prophet of hope in the exile, perhaps later than this prophet, incorporating these poems into the writing of Isaiah 40–55.[4] There has been much discussion over the past century concerning to whom these poems are referring. Suggestions have ranged from an earthly king, the nation of Israel collectively, or a messianic reference to the historical Jesus of Nazareth.

Verses 1-4 describe the character of the Suffering Servant. The word "servant" is translated from the Hebrew word *eved*. This cognate is also attested to in the Ugaritic language for the word "servant," predating the written Hebrew text by at least 500 years. There are five key words describing the servant in verses 1-4. The servant is filled with the spirit of God (v. 1), humble and quiet (v. 2), comforting and encouraging (v. 3), not easily discouraged (v. 4), and a deliverer of justice (v. 4). Before the giving of the Holy Spirit at Pentecost, as recorded in Acts 2, the Old Testament describes the spirit of God coming upon individuals in different times and for differing purposes. The spirit of God in the Old Testament was said to come upon artisans, prophets, political leaders, kings, and here upon the Suffering Servant. The purpose of the Suffering Servant is also identified in verse 1. The servant is to bring justice to the nations. Three times throughout this poem, the servant is said to bring justice (vv. 1, 3, 4).

The Suffering Servant: Poem 2, 49:1-6

The second poem focuses on the specific call of the Suffering Servant. Verses 1-4 say that the servant was called by the God of Israel. The Suffering Servant is described as being called even before his birth. Others have also been identified in the Old Testament as being called before birth. Samson and Jeremiah quickly come to mind (see Judg 13:6-8 and Jeremiah 1:5). It is an abuse of the interpretation of Scripture to make these references into a political strawman. The author of this servant poem is relating issues of the specific call of the servant rather than making twenty-first-century political statements.

I once knew a very kind lady who helped maintain our building. She would be there hours before anyone else darkened the halls of our building each day, cheerfully preparing the classrooms and offices for the work of the upcoming day. As I have the habit of arriving very early each day, I often had interaction with her in the hallways en route to my office. One day we were visiting for a moment and talking about her weekend. I learned that she was a "clogger." For those of you not from southern Appalachia, "clogging" refers to a certain type of dance that is extremely popular with the population of this region. In fact, she turned to me in conversation and said something I will never forget: "You know, Dr. Ballard, I feel like I was born to clog." Ever since she mentioned her self-revelation, I have always thought of her when I read passages throughout the Old Testament referring to being called even before birth. Rather than making these passages into political statements, I have chosen to read them as, simply, "I was born to _____ (fill in the blank)."

The purpose of the call of the Suffering Servant is presented in vv. 5 and 6. First, the Suffering Servant is to call the people of Israel back to God. Presumably, many people had become complacent in their regular worship and religious expression during those years of captivity. The Suffering Servant is to lead the people back to a right relationship with the God of Israel. Second, the Suffering Servant is to be a light to the Gentiles. The love of God is not limited only to the people of Israel or to those who suffered at the hands of the Babylonians. God's love is for all!

The Suffering Servant: Poem 3, 50:4-11

In the third poem of the Suffering Servant, the author now paints a broad portrait of the person who is identified as the Suffering Servant. The author illuminates three vivid and distinct pictures of the life of the coming servant.

First, the reason for the servant is identified in Isaiah 50:1-3. God is sending the Suffering Servant in response to the laments the children of Israel have leveled against God: Why has God divorced us? Why doesn't God act on our behalf? The Suffering Servant is God's response to these serious charges brought against God by the people. In reality, the people had sinned and fallen away from God. The Suffering Servant is needed to redeem or rescue God's people.

Second, the tasks of the servant are identified in vv. 4-9. The Suffering Servant will serve as an ideal learner and teacher (vv. 4-5). The servant will offer himself as a sacrifice on behalf of his people. The servant will offer himself to abuse, but will not be disgraced, because he is aware that his endurance of pain and abasement is part of the purpose for which God has called him.

Third, the outcome of the tasks of the servant is highlighted in vv. 10 and 11. Some will believe the message of the Suffering Servant and will walk in the light. It is literally an altar call of sorts: "Who walks in darkness and has no light, yet trusts in the name of the LORD and relies upon his God?" Unfortunately, there is an opposing side to light. Verse 11 offers a curse upon those who do not trust in the true light of God. Those who oppose the words of the Suffering Servant are called to follow their *own light*, ultimately receiving torment.

The Suffering Servant: Poem Four, 52:13–53:12

The fourth Suffering Servant poem is one of the most influential poems found in literature. Eleven of the twelve verses comprising Isaiah 53 are quoted either entirely or in part throughout the New Testament. All four of the Gospel writers quote at least one verse from this poem. The final Suffering Servant poem is more than just a description of the type of suffering the servant will endure. It is about the Suffering Servant winning the final battle over the evil that brings suffering. It is almost impossible for Christian disciples to read these words and not immediately think of the afflictions of Jesus Christ and what Christ endured during his last few hours on this earth in human form. But I would remind us that this poem has an earlier context and is revered also as Scripture by a separate group of religious adherents who read this poem apart from a Christological interpretation. For practitioners of the Jewish or Christian faith, this poem is a powerful reading of love, sacrifice, and the grace of God.

Isaiah 53:6 is a central text in reading this poem: "All we like sheep have gone astray; we have all turned to our own way, and the Lord has laid on him the iniquity of us all." This central verse reminds us of the human condition. We find ourselves separated from a proper relationship with God due to our own actions. Like the nation of Israel in the exile, we choose to leave God. God does not choose to leave us! In turning away from God, we ultimately try to substitute something in God's place. We each turn to our "own way." The verse also reminds us that we have all chosen to turn away from God at times. But the Suffering Servant makes a way for us to return to God. The outcome of the servant's sacrifice is recorded in v. 12: "He bore the sin of many, and made intercession for the transgressors."

The positioning of these four Suffering Servant poems is crucial to the message of the prophet of hope in the exile. Because of the work of God and God's servant, those living in exile will be redeemed. They will be made whole once again. They will be restored. Even so, the journey is not easy. The years of affliction certainly left a mark on each of their lives. But God does not abandon those who continue to have faith and believe.

Isaiah

A Fitting Farewell to the Prophet of Hope in the Exile, 55:1-13

"Everyone who thirsts, come to the waters; and you that have no money, come, buy and eat! Come, buy wine and milk without money and without price."—Isaiah 55:1

As Isaiah 40:1 encapsulates the spirit of the prophet of hope in the exile, so Isaiah 55:1 represents the spirit of the message of this prophet. An invitation is given to all those in captivity to come, to drink water without payment, and to eat without cost. When Cyrus destroyed Babylon in 539 BCE, the remaining captives of Judah were faced with a choice: Would they stay and maintain their lives in Babylon, or would they return to the land of promise and face uncertainty? God offered these people another opportunity to enter into a covenant relationship with God. The time of exile was over, but the next move was in the hands of the people.

Part Two: Learning How to Live after the Exile, 56–66

The third section of Isaiah, sometimes referred to by scholars as "Trito" or Third Isaiah, describes the writer as back in Jerusalem following the Babylonian captivity. There is ongoing discussion concerning the identity of this prophetic writer. Is this the disciple of the prophet of hope in the exile, or is this the prophet of hope in the exile who is now returned to the land of promise? Or is this an instance of a proleptic nature of Isaiah, the eighth-century prophet simply seeing what is to come? All three positions are possibilities. But of the three I lean toward the position that the writer who penned the words in Isaiah 40–55 is now continuing with a new message for those who have returned to the land of promise. Based on the current state of Isaiah scholarship, I will refer to the author of this section as Third Isaiah.

The call of Third Isaiah is found in Isaiah 61:1-9. In this text the writer/prophet is called to preach good news to the remnant that has returned. The writer/prophet is admonished to care for the hurting who have returned to the land of promise only to find desolation and destruction. The writer/prophet calls them to rebuild what was devastated by the earlier Babylonian invasion and not rebuilt during the exile. Words of hope and blessing also accompany this call. This call also reemphasizes the theme repeated throughout the message of Isaiah 1–39. Isaiah 61:8 states, "For I the LORD love justice, I hate robbery and wrongdoing; I will faithfully give them their recompense, and I will make an everlasting covenant with them."

Motivation for True Worship, 58:1-14

In Isaiah 58, God admonishes Israel because of her sin. The passage indicts Israel for saying they are following God with her lips and then living a different lifestyle than they are professing. In vv. 1-5 Isaiah offers an indictment against the people because of their sin. God calls upon the writer/prophet to cry aloud the sins of Israel. The sin exposed by the writer/prophet is gross hypocrisy. They cry out to God and hold to their acts of penitence and fasting but never allow their relationship with God to transform their lives. They cry out that their acts of worship don't seem to make a difference. Third Isaiah identifies the people's attempt at fasting in public to be disingenuous. God proclaims that religious acts of piety such as public fasting do no good unless they are accompanied by a transformation of the heart. They were guilty of going through the motions without ever experiencing a significant change in their hearts.

In the second half of Isaiah 58, the writer/prophet offers two examples of how the people are to worship. First, the people are instructed on what true fasting really looks like. In vv. 6-12 true fasting is outlined. True fasting should be centered on others and not on our own need and is to be a time of drawing nearer to God. Verses 11-12 add a word of blessing for the person who enters into a fast for God with pure motivation. God promises to meet the person's needs; they will be strengthened, and they will be a rebuilder of broken things. All three of these blessings have particular import for those who returned from the exile. To a people badly in need of hope and encouragement, Third Isaiah reminds them of where true hope lies—not in artificial acts of piety or show, but in true worship with acts of spiritual discipline designed to draw us nearer to God.

The second example of true worship offered by Third Isaiah is found in Isaiah 58:13-14. The people are instructed to honor the Sabbath. Three times in v. 13 they are instructed to make the Sabbath a special day for God. They are not to do their own thing or "what they please." The Sabbath day is the weekly high holy day for the devout person who seeks to practice the Jewish faith. This simple command is foundational in the Ten Commandments. Exodus 20 records more commentary and instruction on this command than any of the other nine commandments. A blessing is also added in Isaiah 58:14 to all who honor the Sabbath by keeping it holy or special. They will find joy in the Lord.

A New Vision for a New Day, 65:17-25

At the end of this lengthy prophetic text, one encounters a beautiful reversal of earlier prophetic warnings. Repeatedly, the Israelites have been warned that if they do not repent and return to the ways of God, they will build homes, but others will live in them; they will plant vineyards, but others will drink of their fruits; they will plant fields of grain, but others will enjoy the harvest. These earlier words of judgment are reversed in this great text. The day of hope has come to Israel. God has not forgotten God's people. Though they have turned from God repeatedly, God is there ready to bless and restore them once again if they will honor the covenant into which they entered. Akin to the ending of Ezekiel, Third Isaiah offers a glimpse into a new day with a new heaven and earth.

Isaiah 65:20 speaks to me in a deeply personal way: "No more shall there be in it an infant that lives but a few days." For the many persons like my wife and I who have endured the death of an infant, this verse offers a word of immeasurable hope and promise. I pray that the day will indeed come where no parent will be in the place of losing a child.[5]

Conclusion

The writings of Isaiah 40–66 bring words of consolation and hope to a people who have longed for a fresh start and a brighter new day. Few texts in the Old Testament offer more pastoral sentiments than those found written by the prophet of hope in the exile. These words offer a sharp contrast to the words found throughout the texts of the eighth-century prophets Amos, Hosea, Micah, and Isaiah of Jerusalem. The words of Isaiah 66:22 are an appropriate benediction to this message of hope: "For as the new heavens and the new earth, which I make, shall remain before me, says the LORD, so shall your descendants and your name remain."

For Further Reading

Blenkinsopp, Joseph. *A History of Prophecy in Israel*. Louisville: Westminster John Knox Press, 1996.

Collins, Jim. *Good to Great*. New York: Harper Business, 2001.

Kelley, Page H. "Isaiah." *The Broadman Bible Commentary*, vol. 5. Nashville: Broadman Press, 1971.

Miller, John W. *Meet the Prophets: A Beginner's Guide to the Books of the Biblical Prophets*. New York: Paulist Press, 1987.

Von Rad, Gerhard. *The Message of the Prophets*. San Francisco: HarperSanFrancisco, 1965.

Watts, John D. W. "Isaiah." *The Prophets: Mercer Commentary on the Bible*, vol. 4. Macon GA: Mercer University Press, 1996.

Webb, Barry. *The Message of Isaiah*. The Bible Speaks Today. Leicester, England: InterVarsity Press, 1997.

Westermann, Claus. *Isaiah 40–66*. The Old Testament Library. Philadelphia: Westminster Press, 1969.

Notes

[1] Page H. Kelley, "Isaiah," in *The Broadman Bible Commentary*, vol. 5 (Nashville: Broadman Press, 1971) 297.

[2] Claus Westermann, *Isaiah 40–66*, The Old Testament Library (Philadelphia: Westminster Press, 1969) 61.

[3] Jim Collins, *Good to Great* (New York: Harper Business, 2001) 85.

[4] Kelley, "Isaiah," 306.

[5] For a detailed description of this event, see Wayne Ballard, "Living with the Pain," in *Assaulted by Grief: Finding God in the Broken Places*, ed. David Crutchley and Gerald Borchert (Jefferson City TN: Mossy Creek Press, 2012).

Chapter 3

Haggai

Throughout my freshman year in high school, my family's life was thoroughly interrupted and put on hold as we endeavored to build the home where my parents still live. My parents acquired a modest acreage that belonged to our Cherokee ancestors during the earlier settlement of the state of Oklahoma. The Great Land Rush of 1889 brought the "white settlers" into the heart of Indian territory with the promise of free land if they could make it as homesteaders. It is a harsh land, where it can be extremely hot and cold and where the wind that comes sweeping over the plains blows ALL the time! Regardless, the land is still special to this day—it is family land. My parents hired a carpenter who worked with us and numerous volunteers (often extended family members) to build the home from the ground up. Every spare moment was spent working on the house. There wasn't much time for anything else in the year of building.

As I read through the two chapters that comprise the text of the short prophetic book called Haggai, I am constantly reminded of that building experience. Haggai has apparently returned to Judah from the Babylonian captivity along with many others. They have all undertaken the tasks of rebuilding their homes, lives, and community. They are all busy, and there is much to do. Haggai steps back and evaluates what is happening during this time and notices that something is missing—the blessings of God. There doesn't appear to have been much fanfare or triumphant celebration when the exiles returned home. There was simply the bitter reality of hard work, labor that must at times have seemed fruitless and overwhelming. Haggai calls the people to rebuild the temple in Jerusalem that was destroyed and is in disarray. Haggai calls the people to look beyond their own concerns and personal situation to the well-being of the community and to return their focus back to the God of their ancestors.

Little is known about this postexilic prophet named Haggai. He is mentioned in two places in the book of Ezra. Ezra 5:1 and 6:14 refer to Haggai, along with Zechariah, crediting them as the impetus behind the building of the second temple. The rebuilding of the temple is important to Haggai as a condition of God's renewed blessing upon the people of his native land. The Hebrew name "Haggai" comes from the root word meaning "festal" or "festival." Some suggest this means that Haggai was born on a Jewish feast or festival day, but this is hardly certain.[1] Haggai, Zechariah, and Malachi represent prophetic voices following the exile during a period described as a time of restoration and hope. These three short prophetic books are closely related and serve as the conclusion to the Minor Prophets, otherwise known as the Book of the Twelve in the Hebrew Bible.

Historical Situation

The book of Haggai offers another example where dating formulas are important to the writer or editor of the texts. Like Ezekiel and Zechariah, there are several specific dates mentioned in a formulaic way throughout this brief message. The superscription to the book begins with a dating formula: "In the second year of King Darius, on the first day of the sixth month." The message of Haggai is set in late summer to late fall of 520 BCE, taking place approximately between August 29 to December 18. There are six different dates given throughout this brief work (1:1, 15; 2:1, 10, 18, 20). The date 520 BCE is significant, as it marks the beginning of work on the second temple, which was completed and rededicated in 515 BCE.

Placing this book in its proper historical contexts allows us to see the panorama behind the words of the text. The days of exile are completed. We have now moved beyond the depiction of captivity described in Ezekiel and Isaiah 40–55. The book of Haggai records the efforts of the postexilic community in rebuilding their lives and rebuilding the temple of Jerusalem in the late sixth century BCE and is akin to the descriptions of life as described in Isaiah 55–66. The prominent world leader mentioned in Haggai 1:1 is Darius, the king of Persia. Darius I reigned in Persia from 521 to 485 BCE, succeeding Cambyses (529–522 BCE). During his early reign Darius was kept busy putting down local rebellions throughout his empire. It appears that he was quite tolerant of the Jewish community that had returned to Palestine during Cyrus's reign. Cyrus is never criticized by the Jews in the Scriptures accredited to this time period.[2]

Zerubbabel and Joshua, mentioned in Haggai 1:1, are the desired recipients of the message of Haggai. Zerubbabel, described as the son of Shealtiel, is the grandson of King Jehoiachin, who reigned in Judah during the first great exilic deportation, which took place in 598 BCE. He is also described as the governor of Judah on behalf of the Persians and is significant because he is also from the line of David. Joshua is identified as the high priest for the postexilic community, responsible for cultic activities and community worship. The message of the restoration of the temple is especially pertinent to Zerubbabel (from the line of David) and Joshua (high priest). David is identified as the patron saint of Israel's worship since the inception of the nation, and 2 Samuel 7 promises that a Davidic heir would sit on the throne of Jerusalem forever. There is clearly high expectation for Zerubbabel by the members of the postexilic community.

The Texts of Haggai

The Call to Action: Rebuild the Temple, 1:1-11

Haggai calls upon the people to begin the work of rebuilding the decimated temple in Jerusalem. Verses 1-3 serve as an introduction to the message of Haggai in a narrative framework that closely resembles superscriptions found in other prophetic texts, yet it retains the purpose for the recording of Haggai's words. As a superscription v. 1 records the king of note in this day, Darius I of Persia, thus giving a historical dating marker from the outset. The verse also establishes the leadership in the postexilic community as Zerubbabel and Joshua. In a classical example of prophetic disputation, v. 2 records that the people have claimed the timing is not right to rebuild the temple. The poetic message in vv. 4-11 outlines God's call to the people to begin the work on the temple.

A starkly contrasting challenge is placed before the people. How can they live in their fine homes with roofs, in comfort, when the house of God lies in ruins? Haggai calls upon the people to look beyond their own circumstances and needs. In vv. 5-6 the people are challenged to consider their own situations. They work and toil, but they never seem to get ahead. The conclusion of v. 6 states, frankly, "You that earn wages earn wages to put them into a bag with holes." These verses are reminiscent of earlier futility curses found in Deuteronomy 28:30-41. These curses are the results of Israel, the covenant people, not keeping the covenant made with the God of their ancestors. The resulting implication states the exilic community is not receiving the expected and needed blessings from God because they have been selfish, putting their own needs before their relationship with God.

In vv. 7-11 the futility curse is expanded as God claims to be taking concerted action in impeding their progress until they willfully turn back to God. The people are instructed to go and retrieve the materials necessary for the rebuilding of the temple and are reminded that God will allow the current hardships to continue until they demonstrate their obedience.

Verse 11 states that God has brought a drought upon the people, the land, the animals, and all their labors. Paronomasia, or Hebrew wordplay, is found in vv. 9-11. While the temple is in ruins (*hareb*), the people will experience drought (*horeb*).

The People Respond, 1:12-15

The text turns again from poetry to narrative in this section, stating that Zerubbabel and Joshua, the leaders of the Jewish postexilic community, have responded favorably to the words of God through the prophet Haggai. Verse 12 uses the term "all the remnant." This term was used often in the exilic writings to refer to the ones who were taken into captivity but would emerge as the new Israel following captivity (compare Jer 43:5). Verse 14 states that the leaders and the people came together to work on the temple of the Lord. It is amazing what takes place when people work together toward a common goal or cause. If you have ever been part of an organization, work environment, or sports team that transcends individuality and personal egos, it can be a memorable experience. Unfortunately, too many people never get to have this type of experience because it just takes one critical voice, or one passing judgment, or one person who wants to be in charge regardless of the existing political structure. Working together for the betterment of all can be a religious experience!

Verse 15 is somewhat problematic in its placement in the Hebrew Text. In the Leningrad Codex, the Hebrew Bible from which most of our English Old Testament texts are translated, this verse is set aside from v. 14 and independent of Haggai 2:1. The question rests upon which section to apply these dates. Is it the final word of chapter 1, or should it be read as the first part of chapter 2? For tradition's sake, I choose to leave it as it rests in most of our texts as the conclusion to chapter 1.

Words of Encouragement and Hope, 2:1-9

The winds of autumn are now in the air. The text of Haggai moves in chapter 1 from August and September into the month of October in 2:1. Once again, vv. 1-2 are narrative, setting up the poetic words that follow in vv. 3-9. Apparently, work on the temple is underway. The prophet Haggai asks, "Who is left among you that saw this house in its former glory? How does it look to you now? Is it not in your sight as nothing?" (v. 3). Haggai calls to mind the grandeur of the former temple built by Solomon. The few remaining survivors who had seen the first temple would have known that the new version paled in comparison to the glory of the previous temple. This could lead to discouragement and the people becoming disheartened. In words reminiscent of God's call to the people through Joshua as recorded in Joshua 1, Haggai calls the leaders and the people to be strong, adding, "Do not fear" (v. 5). We see these words in key intersections throughout the biblical narrative in both the Old and New Testaments. Humanity is frail and given to being fearful, especially at tasks that can often seem overwhelming.

In vv. 6-9 God speaks through Haggai a promise that God will bless the efforts of the people in rebuilding the temple. God promises to fill the temple once again with God's glory, which was said to depart in Ezekiel 10:18. Verses 6-7 describe the action of the return of God's glory as a divine theophany, with God shaking the heavens and the earth. The return of God's glory will be powerful and dramatic, demonstrating the faithfulness and power of God.

Promises of Blessings for Obedience, 2:10-23

Once again, the reader is moved through time to December 520 BCE. Haggai confirms that the blessings of God are coming for the people even though they have defiled themselves. The blessings of God, however, are conditional on the people maintaining a right relationship with God. In vv. 10-14 Haggai outlines that holiness is not transferable to the people just because the temple is restored. Haggai confirms, however, that uncleanness is indeed transferable. When the people allow transgressions to go unchecked, the transgressions affect the entire community. God's promised blessings are conditioned on their obedience to the covenant laid before them.

Verse 18 is a crucial verse in this short witness of Haggai, relating that the rebuilding of the temple marks the beginning of the return of God's glory and God's blessings to the people. Might this relate to the laying of the cornerstone, the chief stone of the new temple? This would have been a symbolic act that certainly would have been accompanied by some ritual observance and ceremony, much like the ribbon-cutting or groundbreaking ceremonies with which we are familiar today. The temple is being rebuilt, and with this the blessings of God will return.

The book of Haggai ends with an eschatological word of hope for Zerubbabel in vv. 20-23. Haggai offers high expectations and hope for Zerubbabel as the leader of the returned exiles. Zerubbabel is referred to by the title "my servant" in v. 23. This title was designated only for the greatest of the Israelite leaders, such Moses, Joshua, and David. There is clearly an air of messianic expectation in these words of Haggai. Haggai also claims that God will make Zerubbabel his "signet ring" in v. 23 as the chosen of the Lord Almighty. Haggai claims a divine favor upon Zerubbabel as the chosen leader. As a bearer of the signet ring of God, Zerubbabel was ascribed God's power and blessing. Haggai ends with words of expectation and hope. The kings of Israel and Judah had failed time and time again to rule in a manner consistent with the covenant of God. Haggai lays great hope at the feet of Zerubbabel as a true messiah who will lead the people back to the ways and blessings of God.

Conclusion

Haggai is a special book, serving as the introduction to the postexilic books of the Minor Prophets of the Old Testament. Haggai calls the people to move beyond their own self-interest to care and invest themselves in the task of rebuilding the Jerusalem temple. This call is also about the unification of the people behind Zerubbabel, a messianic leader who, Haggai believes, will help restore dignity and renewal of the covenant of the people before God. Though a brief book of only two chapters, Haggai is an important example of hope in times of devastation and the power of renewal that is available through faith in God. Faith can move mountains. Faith can unify people with purpose and hope. Faith can bring renewed blessings from God above.

For Further Reading

Ackroyd, Peter R. *Exile and Restoration.* The Old Testament Library. Philadelphia: Westminster Press, 1968.

Berquist, Jon L. "Haggai." *The Prophets: Mercer Commentary on the Bible*, vol. 4. Macon GA: Mercer University Press, 1996.

Bright, John. *A History of Israel.* Philadelphia: Westminster Press, 1981.

Miller, John W. *Meet the Prophets: A Beginner's Guide to the Books of the Biblical Prophets.* New York: Paulist Press, 1987.

Nogalski, James D. *The Book of the Twelve: Micah–Malachi.* Smyth & Helwys Bible Commentary. Macon GA: Smyth & Helwys Publishing, 2011.

Smith, David A. "Haggai." *The Broadman Bible Commentary,* vol. 7. Nashville: Broadman Press, 1972.

Smith, Ralph L. *Micah–Malachi.* Word Biblical Commentary, vol. 32. Waco: Word Books, 1984.

Von Rad, Gerhard. *The Message of the Prophets.* San Francisco: HarperSanFrancisco, 1965.

Notes

[1]Smith, David A. "Haggai," in The Broadman Bible Commentary, vol. 7 (Nashville: Broadman Press, 1972) 291.

[2]James D. Nogalski, The Book of the Twelve: Micah–Malachi, Smyth & Helwys Bible Commentary (Macon GA: Smyth & Helwys Publishing, 2011) 772.

Chapter 4

Zechariah

Zechariah, from the Hebrew *Zakar Ya*, or "Yahweh remembers," is the longest text of the postexilic prophets in the Hebrew canon. Zechariah was a common name in the Old and New Testaments. It applies to thirty different people in the Old Testament and one person in the New Testament. As gathered from its title, one purpose for this prophetic text is to encourage the people of the postexilic period with the news that God has not abandoned them. The foundation for the second temple was laid at the request of Cyrus of Persia under the watchful eye of Sheshbazzar when the exiles were allowed to return in 538 BCE, according to Ezra 5:16. Eighteen years have now passed, and the people are growing anxious. Haggai has stirred the community of the remnant a month or two before the words of Zechariah are given. Unlike Haggai, which is written primarily in third person, Zechariah is written primarily in first person as a personal witness to the details surrounding the rebuilding of the second temple. Zechariah is described as a *navi*, or prophet, a Hebrew word reserved for those who proclaim a message for God. This term is often used throughout the Old Testament opposite of the term *ro'eh*, or seer. Zechariah is also described in v. 1 as the son of Berekiah, the son of Iddo. The book of Ezra identifies Zechariah as the son of Iddo in Ezra 5:1 and 6:14. Iddo is identified as the head of a priestly family who returned, along with Zerubbabel, in

Nehemiah 12:16. Like Ezekiel before him, Zechariah is described as both a prophet and a priest.

Zechariah is a favorite book among the authors of the New Testament. Zechariah 1–8 is often quoted in the apocalyptic literature of the New Testament, especially the book of Revelation. Zechariah 9–14 is quoted throughout the Gospel literature with its emphasis on the messiah as a suffering servant and the kingdom of God understood as a kingdom of service. Like his contemporary Haggai, Zechariah calls for the rebuilding of the Jerusalem temple as a symbol of the people's recommitting of themselves before the God of Israel. Zechariah also describes the two leading public figures, Zerubbabel and Joshua, in messianic terms, helping to elevate the expectations of the postexilic community.

Historical Situation

The writer of Zechariah 1–8 is identified in the text as the prophet Zechariah, a contemporary of Haggai. The superscriptions occurring throughout Zechariah describe the message of this book beginning close to the time of the book of Haggai and continuing over the course of the next two years. Zechariah 1:1 records, "In the eighth month, in the second year of Darius." The Darius mentioned here is Darius I, the Persian king who ruled from 522 to 486 BCE. Zechariah 1:7 records the date of February 519, and 7:1 mentions the date December 518. Thus, Zechariah spans the years of 520 through 518 BCE. The construction of the temple in Jerusalem has begun under the watchful eyes of the land's two dominant leaders, Zerubbabel, described as the governor, and Joshua, the high priest. Zechariah views these two leaders in messianic terms throughout chapters 1–8.

The conditions described in Haggai are also confirmed in the book of Zechariah. The city of Jerusalem is still in need of rebuilding and restoration. The foundation for the temple had been laid two decades earlier, but further construction on the temple was just now underway and would take another five years to complete.

Zechariah

The second part of Zechariah, which includes chapters 9–14, is frequently assigned a later dating in the postexilic period. Scholars have observed the similar landscape portrayed in this text as found in Malachi and selected portions of Isaiah 40–66. John Watts suggests that parts of Zechariah 9-14 may even have a Pre-Exilic background.[1] This period suggests a time when the initial enthusiasm for the rebuilding and dedication of the Jerusalem temple had long been forgotten. The remnant had fallen back into a pattern of business as usual, and these prophetic writers remind the people that they have forgotten the hard lessons their God was trying to teach them through the experience of the exile. The keeping of the covenant with the God of their forefathers is rewarded, but breaking the covenant is punished with calamity. The overall sense of malaise or futility precisely correlates to their commitment to their covenantal relationship with God.

Understanding the Two Divisions

Much like the issues surrounding the writing of the text of Isaiah, scholars generally assume that there are two separate parts of the book of Zechariah. Zechariah 1–8 is characterized as apocalyptic writing, taking great pains to use symbolic language and images to deliver the author's intended message. Zechariah 9–14, on the other hand, generally weaves older prophetic themes into a new message for the postexilic community. Joseph Mede suggested as early as 1638 that Zechariah 1–8 and 9–14 were written by separate authors. In Matthew 27:9-11 the author quotes from Zechariah 11:12-13 but credits the words to Jeremiah, suggesting that even in the days of the writing of the New Testament, the authorship of Zechariah 9–14 was uncertain.

The Persian background so prominent in Zechariah 1–8 is nonexistent in 9–14. The peaceful conditions described in the time of Zerubbabel in 1–8 are now gone, replaced with political turmoil and upheaval in 9–14. Greece, the next world superpower after Persia, is mentioned by name in 9:13. The leaders Zerubbabel and Joshua, who were favored so prominently in 1–8, are wholly missing in 9–14. They are replaced with generic descriptions of shepherds as the leaders of the postexilic community.2

There is another reason why scholars see two separate, independent parts to the book of Zechariah. When one encounters the text of Zechariah 9–14 in the Hebrew language, one can see a direct connection to the book of Malachi, which follows in the Book of the Twelve. There is a titular word in the Hebrew text preceding Zechariah 9:1. The word Hebrew word *massa'*, often translated as "oracle" or "message," is set apart in 9:1 as a heading. In Zechariah 12:1 the word *massa'* is the first word of the verse, but it is not set apart from the text in titular form. Again, Malachi 1:1 begins with the word *massa'*. Knowledge of the Hebrew texts also pays dividends in understanding this construction. Malachi in the English versions is comprised of four chapters, but in the Hebrew Bible Malachi is only three chapters, with the six verses found in chapter 4 in the English text serving as the ending of chapter 3 in the Hebrew text. Thus, when one takes a bird's-eye view to the second half of Zechariah and the book of Malachi, one sees three sections of three chapters, each beginning with the Hebrew word *massa'*. The name Malachi in Hebrew also translates as "my messenger." Scholars who specialize in the study of the Book of the Twelve have long noticed this possibility of Zechariah 9–14 and Malachi being written by the same author describing conditions in a later period than is described in Zechariah 1–8.

The Texts of Zechariah

Part One: Apocalyptic Visions of Zechariah, Son of Berekiah, 1–8

Zechariah focuses on two major points in his message: the temple and the messianic age. Like Haggai, Zechariah preaches the rebuilding of the Jerusalem temple will usher in a time of God's renewed presence with Israel. Once the temple is rebuilt, Zechariah believed the messianic age would soon follow.

Zechariah 1:1-6

The book of Zechariah opens with a clear, concise message: "Return to me, says the LORD of hosts, and I will return to you" (v. 3). This message also reappears in Malachi 3:7, and the theme of covenant renewal runs throughout the postexilic thread of Old Testament texts, especially in the Minor Prophets. The verb commonly translated as "repent/return," *shuv*, is found eighteen times in the book of Zechariah.[3] Zechariah admonishes the people to go beyond the religious faithlessness of their forefathers, who did not listen to the earlier prophets. Though no specific texts are addressed, the reference to earlier prophets could refer to the whole body of existing prophetic literature of the time or perhaps to those prophets who presented a message to the people leading up to the exile.

Zechariah 1:7–6:15

Throughout this body of texts, Zechariah utilizes a type of literature described as "vision" literature. These visions, for the most part, follow the same pattern in their literary development. First, Zechariah describes what he has witnessed. Second, Zechariah asks a question about what he just witnessed. Finally, an interpretation is given by an angel or divine being. These visions remind the reader of the visions found in Ezekiel, and they are considered one of the earliest apocalyptic bodies of literature in the Old Testament. But unlike many other apocalyptic texts, Zechariah does not personally deliver the oracles, but rather reports what he claims as angelic interpretation of these visions.

Zechariah continues his prophetic message with a series of eight visions. The first vision, found in 1:7-17, records Zechariah witnessing four horses of differing colors with four riders. They have been patrolling the earth and have found that the world is generally at peace. The angel laments as a sign that God's judgment and salvation have not yet come. The vision is meant to encourage the reader that the day of God's salvation is close at hand. God will restore Jerusalem, and the enemies of Israel will be ultimately defeated. The second vision, 1:18-20, records the destruction of the enemies of Israel, represented by four horns who have oppressed Israel. Zechariah 2:1-13, the third vision, sees a man who is measuring Jerusalem who is stopped in his work. Jerusalem will now be a city without walls, where God protects the city with a "wall of fire" (2:5). Those who are still in exile in places outside of the land of Israel are encouraged to return and enjoy the safety offered by the God of Israel in their homeland in vv. 6-13.

The fourth vision in this collection of visions, Zechariah 3:1-10, varies from the aforementioned pattern. Zechariah is now witness to a divine assembly. This scene is repeated infrequently in the Old Testament (compare to Job 1:6 and following verses). A common thread of these scenes is the presence of God, a divine assembly of angelic beings, and a figure known as *hasatan* in Hebrew, literally, "the accuser." Though simply translated as "Satan" in most English texts, this translation is somewhat misleading for most readers. It is a figure that seemingly has open access to the heavenly council and speaks freely in this assembly.[4] In this vision Zechariah sees Joshua, the high priest, before the divine assembly, being accused by the figure simply identified as Satan, or the accuser. In this scene God rebukes the accuser, calling for fresh clothes and a clean turban to be placed upon Joshua. In one sense the scene is reminiscent of the ancient covenant renewal ceremony witnessed first in Joshua 24. It symbolizes the need for the people of the postexilic community to purify themselves and recommit to the covenant of their forefathers. Verses 8-10 relate that the purification of Joshua, and as a result the people of God, ushers the people to the time of a coming messiah. The word "branch," found in v. 8, reminds the reader of the description of this coming figure used by Isaiah in Isaiah 11:1. The word "servant" also reminds the reader of the Suffering

Servant poems located in Isaiah 40–55, which also have clear messianic overtones.

The fifth vision is located in Zechariah 4:1-14 and, like the previous vision, has messianic overtones. This vision sees Joshua and Zerubbabel being portrayed as two olive trees standing beside a golden lampstand. They are charged with providing a constant supply of oil for this stand. God is represented by the lampstand accompanying Joshua and Zerubbabel, representing the priests and royal servants, respectively. This vision anticipates the completion of the Jerusalem temple. The people are reminded that the temple will be completed not by the work of the people alone but with God's oversight. Verse 6 reports, "Not by might, nor by power, but my spirit, says the LORD." Throughout this vision both Zerubbabel and Joshua are seen as dual messianic figures. This messianic portrayal precedes the anticipation of dual messianic figures representing royalty and priestly concerns as evidenced in later texts found in the Qumran community, also known as the Dead Sea Scrolls.

The sixth and seventh visions are found in Zechariah 5:1-4 and 5:5-11. In the sixth vision Zechariah sees a flying scroll, described as thirty feet long and fifteen feet wide. The scroll is said to represent a word from God against perjurers and thieves. The picture represents the purification of the postexilic community in preparation for the coming of the messianic kingdom. The seventh vision opens with a basket coming toward Zechariah. Inside the basket is a woman, who represents wickedness. The basket is whisked away by two winged women who carry the basket to Babylon, where it will be worshiped in a temple there. Like the sixth vision, this vision represents the cleansing of the land in preparation of the messianic age. It also chastises those Jews who still remained in Babylon and decided not to return to the land of Judah following the decree by Cyrus allowing the exiled peoples to return to their homelands. The final of these eight visions is recorded in 6:1-8. There is much scholarly disagreement upon the meaning of the symbolism found in this vision, but it also speaks of the coming of the messianic age.

Zechariah 7–8

Zechariah 7 begins with another dating formula, providing the reader with the time of November 518 BCE. An envoy from Bethel addresses the priests with a question: Is it right for the people to continue to fast and mourn for the destruction of the first temple? God directs Zechariah to respond. The mode of spiritual practice is unimportant, but what is in the heart really matters. Zechariah redirects the people to the heart of the eighth-century message of Amos, Hosea, Micah, and Isaiah, who all centered their messages on the concept of social justice. Micah 6:8 and Amos 5:24 are great examples of this message. God isn't concerned with the religious drizzle or show. God desires a pure heart that manifests itself with action for the poor, the needy, the widow, and the orphan. Zechariah 7:9-10 states, "Render true judgments, show kindness and mercy to one another; do not oppress the widow, the orphan, the alien, or the poor; and do not devise evil in your hearts against one another." Zechariah 8 is a declaration of God's promises to bless Jerusalem in the coming days. The messianic age is coming. With these words, the ministry of Zechariah the postexilic prophet apparently ends. He, along with Haggai, offers words of encouragement, hope, and expectation for a community that is downtrodden and tired. There is much excitement concerning Zerubbabel and Joshua as co-messianic figures for this community. But, alas, this expectation does not last long. The outcome of Zerubbabel is lost forever to the pages of history. Did the Persians remove him as governor when such messianic expectation arose in Jerusalem? Or did he simply live out his days without reaching the lauds afforded him by Haggai and Zechariah? Unfortunately, we may never know. Ezra 5:2 and perhaps Ezra 6:7 are the last known references to Zerubbabel. Like Zerubbabel, enthusiasm faded among the people. Even the rebuilding and rededication of the temple did little to energize or renew the faith of the people of Israel. All the expectation and enthusiasm eventually ceased.

ZECHARIAH

Part Two: Oracles of Second Zechariah, 9–14

Zechariah 9–14 is probably the result of writing long after the days of the prophet Zechariah so prominent in Zechariah 1–8. There are, however, a number of similar themes that run concurrently throughout the first part of Zechariah that are also repeated in chapters 9–14. The promise of a new Jerusalem is found in both parts of the book (2:4-5; 14:8-11). The return of the exiles is also a common theme throughout Zechariah (8:6-8; 10:6-10). God's judgment over all people, including the foreign nations, is another theme in both sections (2:1-2; 14:16). The ongoing cleansing of the land from iniquity and sin is found in first and second Zechariah (5:1-11; 13:1-2). And one more theme that appears in both Zechariah 1–8 and 9–14 is the appearance of a humble messianic figure (3:8; 4:6; 9:9-10).

Zechariah 9–14 is often quoted throughout the New Testament. In fact, it is the most quoted Old Testament text during the Gospels' description of the Passion Narrative. Jesus' identity as Messiah was also shaped from these words. The table found below records a list of the quotations and allusions of Zechariah 9–14 and its corresponding New Testament reference.

This evidence leaves little doubt that Zechariah 9–14 was interpreted messianically by the first-century Christian community.

Zechariah	**New Testament Reference**
9:9	Matthew 21:5; John 12:15
11:13	Matthew 27:9
12:3	Luke 21:24
12:10	John 19:37; Revelation 1:7
13:7	Mark 14:27; Matthew 26:31
14:5	1 Thessalonians 3:13
14:8	John 7:38
14:21	John 2:16

Zechariah 9–11

The first oracle, or *massa'*, begins with the judgment of the enemies of Israel in Zechariah 9:1-8. Syria (Damascus), Phonecia (Tyre and Sidon), and the Philistines (Ashkelon, Gaza, Ekron, and Ashdod) will all be defeated by the "word of the Lord." Verse 8 offers the promise of God's protection for the land of Israel: "Then I will encamp at my house as a guard, so that no one shall march to and fro; no oppressor shall again overrun them, for now I have seen with my own eyes." Bernhard Stade argued in 1881 that the context for the writing of Zechariah 9–14 followed the death of Alexander the Great, of the Greek Empire, when his generals struggled for power in the late fourth century BCE, close to 300 BCE. Those who have traditionally followed Stade's idea see the destruction as these three nations corresponding to the march south of Alexander the Great as a symbol of God's strength over the enemies of Israel. Gath, the fifth major Philistine city-state, is omitted in this list of Philistine city-states.

Zechariah 9:9-10 is one of the most beloved passages in the book of Zechariah. It is directly quoted in Matthew 21:5 and John 12:15 in connection to the triumphal entry of Jesus at the beginning of the Passion Narrative. This messianic figure will enter Jerusalem on a donkey, a symbol of royalty in ancient Israel (Gen 49:11; Judg 5:10; 12:14). Zechariah describes a humble messiah who will reunite Ephraim (the northern tribes) and Judah (the southern tribes) and usher in an age of peace.

A divine theophany is described in Zechariah 9:11-17 as the God of Israel appears as a divine warrior in the storm clouds, leading Israel into a war against the enemies of Israel. God is often portrayed throughout the Old Testament as a divine warrior who brings about peace only after defeating the enemies of God, who are often reflective of Israel's enemies.[5] Zechariah 10:1–11:3 outlines God's care for the people of Israel, expressing God's dismay for how the foreign rulers have treated God's people. God promises to raise up new leaders for Israel during this time from within the nation of Israel herself

(v. 4). Using the term "Judah" in v. 4 is a clear reference to the Davidic succession promised in 2 Samuel 7 (as long as there was a nation of Israel, a Davidic heir would inhabit the throne).

Zechariah 11:4-17 concludes this body of the texts with an allegory of a shepherd and his flock. The shepherd is given instructions to shepherd the flock that is destined for slaughter. The shepherd cares for his flock with two staffs, named "favor" and "union." The shepherd breaks the staff, favor, symbolizing the covenant the people had broken with their God. The shepherd is paid thirty pieces of silver, but he subsequently tosses it into the potter's field upon the Lord's instruction. This is explained as the value the people have placed upon their shepherd and, by extension, the value they have placed upon the God of Israel. The shepherd then breaks the second staff, union, symbolizing the union between Israel (northern tribes) and Judah (southern tribes). The passage ends with God promising to send a shepherd, who is described as "worthless," who will desert the flock. The meaning of this allegory accuses the people of being disobedient and unworthy of God's care or God's rule. This allegory seems out of place when one recalls the upbeat words of encouragement in Zechariah 1–8 unless it is indeed indicative of another author, time, and place.

Zechariah 12–14

The second oracle, or *massa'*, begins with God's defense of Jerusalem against "all the nations of the earth." Once again, God will raise up the Davidic dynasty. Verse 10 states that the nations will mourn over a slain messianic figure "as one mourns for an only child." There are clear connections being made by the author of this text back to the descriptions of the Suffering Servant who is pierced for their transgressions and bruised for their iniquities (Isa 40–55). Zechariah 13:1-6 pictures a fountain opening up to cleanse the people of impurity and idolatry. Prophecy will also cease to exist. The prophets had become corrupt and are accused of deceiving the people.

Zechariah 13:7-9 vividly portrays God's shepherd, a messianic figure, being struck down, along with two-thirds of the population. Once again, however, a remnant, or about one-third, will be delivered, purified, and once again called God's people.

Zechariah 14 offers a conclusion to this second "oracle" of Zechariah. Like many books that utilize apocalyptic writing, the book concludes with a picture of the coming reign of God. Jerusalem will once again be attacked by the nations of the world. The attack will be successful, and the city will be plundered. The author goes into vivid detail of the horrors of this event. The God of Israel does respond, leading out once again as the divine warrior against the rival nations of the world. Creating an image rivaling those of ancient Greek mythology, the God of Israel stands on the Mount of Olives across the valley from Jerusalem, splitting the Mount of Olives into two pieces, initiating and establishing God's reign on earth. Verse 9 recounts, "And the LORD will become king over all the earth; on that day the LORD will be one and his name one." Jerusalem will now be eternally secure. Verses 12-16 describe a great plague that will afflict the people. To the delight of young people everywhere at the beginning of the twenty-first century, there is an ancient biblical description that could be loosely identified as a "zombie apocalypse"!

The remainder of chapter 14 details the future celebration of the Feast of Tabernacles, or Booths. Called by the Hebrew word *Sukkoth*, the feast was instituted as a celebration commemorating the deliverance of the Israelites in the wilderness when escaping from the Egyptians during the time of exodus. During this time of duress and affliction, God provided manna, quail, and water for them as well as divine protection and guidance along the way. Over the centuries it has been celebrated in differing ways. But the basis for the celebration, which is a fall harvest festival, is a time for the celebrant to "re-create" the wilderness experience by constructing a tent or lean-to and spending at least one night in this temporary dwelling as a reminder of God's loving provision.

Though I am not of Jewish ancestry, my wife and I have our own way of remembering the Feast of the

Tabernacles. In 1987 we loaded up two pickups and a Chevrolet Citation and headed to the Bay Area of California to attend Golden Gate Baptist Theological Seminary. Along the way we had to replace four tires on my wife's car. The transmission on my Nissan pickup also had to be repaired. When we finally arrived in California, we had enough money to pay for my fall matriculation to seminary and for one month's rent in the seminary married housing. We also had one package of navy beans. Neither of us liked navy beans, but at her grandmother's suggestion, Kim has always kept a bag of beans in the cabinet for emergencies. Furthermore, we had no jobs waiting upon our arrival. We checked out the campus job board, and my wife was fortunate enough to be hired by a kind Jewish lady who managed a personal accounting firm primarily catering to musicians in the Bay Area. I also was rescued by the First Baptist Church of Novato as a part-time youth pastor. That bag of navy beans lasted us until we received our first paychecks. Now, every time I eat a navy bean, I smile and fondly remember a time when we trusted God and God delivered us from starvation and failure—in spite of our best efforts! If you have never personally experienced a time of deliverance, my prayer for you is that God will allow you the honor of experiencing the uplifting grace of God in your own life!

Conclusion

Zechariah is a diverse book. It was written to call the people of Israel to a renewed vision and hope. The words of Zechariah call its readers back to a renewed faith to God. The very name Zechariah, *Zakar Ya*, reminds the postexilic community that they have not been forgotten or abandoned by God—Yahweh remembers!

For Further Reading

Ackroyd, Peter R. *Exile and Restoration.* The Old Testament Library. Philadelphia: Westminster Press, 1968.

Ballard, Harold W. *The Divine Warrior Motif in the Psalms* (Richland Hills TX: The Berkeley Institute of Biblical and Archaeological Literature, 1999).

Berquist, Jon L. "Zechariah." *The Prophets: Mercer Commentary on the Bible*, vol. 4. Macon GA: Mercer University Press, 1996.

Bright, John. *A History of Israel*. Philadelphia: Westminster Press, 1981.

Miller, John W. *Meet the Prophets: A Beginner's Guide to the Books of the Biblical Prophets*. New York: Paulist Press, 1987.

Nogalski, James D. *The Book of the Twelve: Micah–Malachi*. Smyth & Helwys Bible Commentary. Macon GA: Smyth & Helwys Publishing, 2011.

Smith, Ralph L. *Micah–Malachi*. Word Biblical Commentary, vol. 32. Waco: Word Books, 1984.

Watts, John D. W. "Zechariah." *The Broadman Bible Commentary*, vol. 7. Nashville: Broadman Press, 1972.

West, James King. *Introduction to the Old Testament*. New York: Macmillan Publishing Company, 1981.

Notes

[1] John D. W. Watts, "Zechariah," in *The Broadman Bible Commentary*, vol. 7 (Nashville: Broadman Press, 1972) 309.

[2] James King West, *Introduction to the Old Testament* (New York: Macmillan Publishing Company, 1981) 420–23.

[3] James D. Nogalski, *The Book of the Twelve: Micah–Malachi*, Smyth & Helwys Bible Commentary (Macon GA: Smyth & Helwys Publishing, 2011) 825.

[4] For a detailed description of Satan in biblical literature, see Nogalski, *Micah–Malachi*, 846.

[5] For a detailed discussion of the God of Israel as a divine warrior, see my dissertation, *The Divine Warrior Motif in the Psalms* (Richland Hills TX: The Berkeley Institute of Biblical and Archaeological Literature, 1999).

Chapter 5

Malachi

Malachi is the final book in the Old Testament in the Christian canon. Malachi 4 ends with the promise of the coming of Elijah to precede the coming Day of the Lord, sometimes interpreted as the arrival of the messiah. This ending fits nicely into the Christian canon, coinciding with the arrival of John the Baptist in Matthew 3 and providing the way for Jesus of Nazareth, who is clearly the long-awaited Messiah, according to Matthew's understanding of who Jesus is and what has been declared by the Jewish prophets of old. But with a hushed question, one must step back from this facile interpretation and quietly remember a simple truth. The Hebrew canon does not end with the book of Malachi. In the Hebrew canon, the three major divisions include the *Torah*, or Law; the *Nevi'im*, or Prophets; and the *Ketuvim*, or Writings. Thus, Malachi does end the texts attributed to the prophets of Israel, but the end of the Hebrew Bible rests with 2 Chronicles 36 and the proclamation by Cyrus, king of Persia, who has decreed that the Jerusalem temple will be rebuilt. It is perhaps fitting that the final book of the prophets of the Old Testament points to the coming Day of the Lord, but there is much more to Malachi than just serving as a witness to the coming of the messiah.

In Hebrew, *Malachi* means "my messenger." There is no mention of an Israelite prophet bearing this name apart from this book. The title in the Septuagint, or Greek translation, of

Malachi is *Malacho*. The change of the ending of this word changes the meaning from "my" to "his" messenger. This may reflect the early Jewish understanding of the anonymous nature of this author. This coincides with the aforementioned literary connection between Zechariah 9–11 and 12–14, as Malachi also begins with the Hebrew word *massa'*, meaning "oracle" or "message." Though we know almost nothing about the identity of the author of Malachi, the book does have great merit in the Old Testament witness and calls its readers to move beyond the apathy of their day into a day of authentic faith once again in the God of Israel.

Apathy has become a dominant theme of the people toward their faith and the God of Israel. Malachi describes the state of marriage as being in woeful disrepair. Jewish men were divorcing their Jewish wives in favor of non-Jewish wives, placing them in danger of repeating the mistakes of King Solomon—following the religious practices of foreign gods (Mal 2:10-16). People were also becoming flippant with their commitment to providing for the needs of the temple and the priests by not paying their tithes and offerings to the temple (Mal 1:7-14; 3:8-10). The priesthood itself had become guilty of becoming corrupt and irrelevant to the needs of their day (2:1-9). The writer of Malachi responds to this general apathy by issuing a call back to the worship of the God of Israel.

Malachi employs a unique literary style for its prophetic word. The main body of this brief book is a collection of six disputation speeches (1:2-5; 1:6–2:9; 2:10-16; 2:17–3:5; 3:6-12; 3:13–4:13). Each disputation speech begins with a premise, featuring a misgiving on Israel's part. A question is then posed from the point of view of the people in question. The author then provides an answer to the question, citing the guilt of the people. Through this literary style, the author is offering words of hope and necessary correction. The author emphasizes the changes needed by the community in order to please God.

MALACHI

Historical Situation

Malachi has proven problematic for scholars trying to provide a date and historical background for this writing. Unlike many of the prophetic texts, the superscription in Malachi 1:1 does not identify a time of the message with a monarch of the ancient Near East, nor is there a connection with a prominent name in Israelite history. There are subtle clues throughout the book that can aid in providing a working theory for the time and place of the writing. The second temple is mentioned in 1:10, 3:1, and 3:10 and presumably in use, making the writing of the book later than 515 BCE, when the second temple was dedicated. Malachi 1:8 refers to a governor using a Persian loan word for this designation, perhaps referring to a governor appointed by one of the Persian rulers in this time period. The Persian rulers following the dedication of the second temple include Darius I (522–486 BCE), Xerxes (486–465 BCE), and Artaxerxes (465–424 BCE). The conditions described throughout the book of Malachi are also similar to what one encounters in the books of Ezra and Nehemiah in the late fifth century BCE. Nehemiah leads in the institutional reforms first mentioned in the book of Malachi (compare Mal 3:5 and Neh 5:1-13; Mal 2:10-16 and Neh 13:23-29; Mal 3:7-10 and Neh 10:37-39). The optimism so prominent in Haggai and Zechariah has evaporated. Spiritual apathy and malaise are the dominant terms used to describe the religious devotion of the people throughout Malachi. The people were pessimistic toward the belief that their God was the true God since this belief didn't seem to impact the betterment of their lives. Corruption was prominent among the community leaders and especially among the priests. Though speculative at best, 500–450 BCE is generally agreed upon by scholars today as a date for the writing and background of Malachi.

The Texts of Malachi

Malachi 1:1

This brief superscription attributes this work to Malachi, "my messenger," through the word of the Lord. Like Zechariah 9:1 and 12:1, it begins with the word *massa'*. The Septuagint reads slightly different than the Hebrew text: "The oracle of the word of the LORD to Israel by the hand of his angel." The Targum of Jonathan adds the phrase "by Malachi, *whose name is Ezra the scribe.*"[1] Whether read as "my messenger" or "his messenger," it is clear that God has a message for the people of this day who have become complacent with their religious commitments.

Malachi 1:2-5

The first disputation speech centers upon the love of God for Israel. Verse 2 begins with the affirmation of God's love for Israel. Through years of struggle, however, the people of Israel have turned from God, questioning the premise of God's love for them. This question had plagued the people of Israel beginning with the time of the exodus. How quickly we can forget the wonderful activities and blessings of God. In essence, the people were asking about the relevancy of God. The prophet calls the readers to ponder the fate of their brothers, the Edomites, who have now been destroyed. As the descendants of Esau, God proclaims God's love for the Israelites and God's rejection of the Edomites. From the outset Malachi outlines both God's salvation and judgment. The prophet reminds the people that God had pruned their ranks through the great exile, but now restoration had happened while the Edomites had not been restored. One could compare the words of Malachi here as leading the people in the recitation of the familiar hymn "Count Your Blessings."

Lamentations 4:21-22 records the coming judgment pronounced upon the Edomites during the captivity of Jerusalem. The Edomites are castigated for turning a blind eye to the fate of their brother Israel and, even worse, for taking part in the plunder of Jerusalem during its fall. The book of Obadiah also speaks of the judgment coming for the Edomites. These same Edomites, later known by the name Idumeans by the time of the New Testament, settled in the land of southern Palestine, congregating around the city of Hebron. The family of Herod the Great were descendants of the Edomites.[2]

Malachi 1:6–2:9

God demands our best. Proper respect and fear of God is at the heart of the second disputation speech. The prophet indicts the priests for offering blemished animal offerings before God. The priests are accused of bringing sacrificial animals with defects, withholding the best of the flocks from God. The Mosaic Law called for unblemished animals to be used in sacrifice (Lev 22:20-22). Verse 6 describes the God of Israel in terms of fatherhood. God as father is mentioned explicitly four other times in the Old Testament (Ex 4:22; Deut 32:6; Isa 63:16; 64:8). The prophet asks where respect for the father of the people can be found.

    The prophet calls for immediate action on the part of the priest, even wishing for the temple doors to be closed in v. 10 rather than allowing the defilement by the priests to continue. No service at all is preferred to lackadaisical attempts at pleasing God. In v. 14 a curse is offered against anyone who knowingly offers a blemished sacrifice when they have the means to do otherwise. This is a terrible reproof against the priesthood, but it is also a broader rebuff against the entire group of people.

Malachi 2:10-16

The third disputation speech of Malachi speaks to the covenant the Israelites have broken with God. Like many other classical prophets before, infidelity to the covenant of marriage is used as an allegory to further the prophet's message. But perhaps unlike some previous examples that may have been purely didactic, the message of Malachi speaks to the actual institution of marriage that is being violated by the people of Israel. The people have not only abandoned their commitment to the God of their forefathers; they have also abandoned their commitment to each other. It appears from this passage that Jewish men were divorcing their Jewish wives in favor of foreign wives. Verse 14 directly relates marriage as a similar covenant between men and their wives and the people of Israel with God. The people of Israel have been unfaithful in both instances.

Malachi 2:17–3:5

The justice of God and its relationship to the coming Day of the Lord is the subject of the next disputation speech. The people are questioning the justice of God in verse 17. Why does evil often go unpunished? This theme is also explored in Psalms 37 and 73. In both of these psalms, the author states disgust with the prosperity of the wicked over against the suffering of the righteous. Both psalms respond ultimately that the wicked will not prosper at the end of the day. God is just, and justice will prevail.

The implication in Malachi's message is that the people are being treated justly because of their unfaithfulness. They are not experiencing the blessings of God because of their lack of attention to their covenant with God. The prophet exclaims that a day of justice is coming in the Day of the Lord. This is the only place in the Old Testament where a messenger is described as coming to prepare the people for this time of judgment. The messenger who comes before this day will begin the work of the purification of the priesthood, the temple, and the sacrificial system.

This question is asked frequently in our world today. How do we answer our friends and neighbors who ask us this difficult question? Where was God during the Holocaust? Where is God in the great natural catastrophes of our day? The tsunamis, the earthquakes, the floods, the volcanoes all seem to point to a God who is powerless to act on behalf of human history or events. Time does not permit for a fuller discussion of the concept of theodicy at this point. Theodicy simply refers to the following question: If God is good and all-powerful, then why does evil exist, and why do so many innocent people suffer? A Christological response to these questions is that the justice of God has been restored in the person of Jesus Christ. Mercy, grace, and justice are now possible through a personal relationship with Jesus of Nazareth.

Malachi 3:6-12

The fifth disputation speech details the manner the people have robbed God through withholding the giving of their tithes and offerings. In Malachi 3:6-7 a great theological truth is set forth. God is immutable—in other words, God does not change. This same concept of God is also restated in the New Testament in Hebrews 13:8 in reference to Jesus. The people are reminded that God has not left them; they have left God. Though the people have repeatedly abandoned the covenant they first made with God at Sinai, God constantly and repeatedly stands ready to renew the covenant with God's people. Verse 7b is a revivalistic challenge: "Return to me, and I will return to you."

The people challenge the premises set forth in Malachi's message: "How do we rob God?" (v. 8). God responds to the people, reminding them that they have withheld their tithes and offerings for the working of the temple. The people are offered a challenge. They are to bring their tithes and offerings to the temple to see if God will indeed bless them once again, rewarding their faithfulness.

Like the picture of the patient father in the story of the prodigal son in Luke 15:20-14, God stands patiently, waiting for the people of the postexilic community to once again turn to God for sustenance and life. When God's people turn to God, they can expect once again to find renewed grace, renewed pardon, renewed life, and a renewed heart.

Malachi 3:13–4:3

A charge is made against the people for speaking harshly against their God. The people doubt God's relevance to their daily lives, and in turn they have abandoned the pursuit of pleasing God. Some did fear God and continued to encourage one another in the ways of faithfulness. The prophet speaks of a Book of Remembrance, where the names of these faithful have been written by God's own hand. The faithful will be spared on the terrible Day of the Lord. The wicked will be burnt by the coming fire of judgment. The righteous, however, will spring forth like young calves from a stall just opened, enthusiastically entering into the unforeseen future, living by faith in the God of Israel. Joel 2:30-31 speaks of the Day of the Lord as a day of judgment complete with fire and smoke. God's destruction will be complete, and no one who has rejected God will be able to escape.

Malachi 4:4-6

Malachi 4 concludes with two short appendices. The first appendix is located in v. 4. The people are encouraged to remember the Law of Moses. The Septuagint moves this verse to the end of Malachi 4, leaving this emphasis on keeping the Law as the last word of Malachi. Paul describes the Law as a mirror in Galatians 3:19-25. The Law is given as a means for keeping the covenant between Israel and God. Israel kept the covenant by keeping the Law. Israel broke the covenant by breaking the Law. God has never been a cosmic "killjoy." The Law, in many ways, is a reflection of God's grace. God gave the people a mechanism that can be used to maintain a proper relationship with God. Unfortunately, no one is able to keep the Law perfectly. For members of the Christian faith, the Law is the preparation for humanity's learning to live in relationship with God. Jesus Christ was not Plan B because Plan A (the Law) failed. Jesus Christ was Plan A from the beginning. The call to remember the Law is a call to remember the very grace of God.

The second appendix, found in Malachi 4:5-6, speaks to the return of Elijah as a precursor to the coming Day of the Lord. Elijah is a pivotal religious figure in the history of the Israelite people. Second Kings 2:11-12 records the ascension of Elijah into the heavens; thus, he was assumed to never have died physically, but rather he was taken into the heavens in order to return, at least figuratively, in preparation for the coming Day of the Lord. The Christian tradition assumes the return of Elijah to be complete in the person of John the Baptist, who prepares the way for the coming of the public ministry of Jesus Christ.

Conclusion

The final book of the Book of the Twelve, the *Nevi'im*, and the conclusion of the Christian canon of the Old Testament, Malachi may be only four chapters long, but it is a major contributor to the overall message of the Old Testament. Its rich disputation style, unique in the Old Testament, along with its mystery of authorship and provenance make it a joy to read and study. It speaks to persons of faith today, calling us to reevaluate our motivation for worship, service, and life. Are we ever like the postexilic community of Israel, guilty of robbing God by withholding our tithes and offerings? Are we guilty of breaking the covenant we have made with God through the lack of attention we pay to our relationship to Jesus Christ? Have we ever been guilty of offering God less than the best we have? These disputations are pointed questions as we reflect on our own lives today. May God richly bless your reading and studying of these words, and may you one day read that your name is written in the Book of Remembrance (3:16).

For Further Reading

Ackroyd, Peter R. *Exile and Restoration*. The Old Testament Library. Philadelphia: Westminster Press, 1968.

Bennett, T. Miles. "Malachi." *The Broadman Bible Commentary*, vol. 7. Nashville: Broadman Press, 1972.

Berquist, Jon L. "Malachi." *The Prophets: Mercer Commentary on the Bible*, vol. 4. Macon GA: Mercer University Press, 1996.

Miller, John W. *Meet the Prophets: A Beginner's Guide to the Books of the Biblical Prophets*. New York: Paulist Press, 1987.

Nogalski, James D. *The Book of the Twelve: Micah–Malachi*. Smyth & Helwys Bible Commentary. Macon GA: Smyth & Helwys Publishing, 2011.

Smith, Ralph L. *Micah–Malachi*. Word Biblical Commentary, vol. 32. Waco: Word Books, 1984.

Von Rad, Gerhard. *The Message of the Prophets*. San Francisco: HarperSanFrancisco, 1965.

West, James King. *Introduction to the Old Testament*. New York: Macmillan Publishing Company, 1981.

Notes

[1] T. Miles Bennett, "Malachi," in *The Broadman Bible Commentary*, vol. 7 (Nashville: Broadman Press, 1972) 366.

[2] Bennett, "Malachi," 1972.

Chapter 6

1 & 2 Chronicles

Imagine that someone is presently reading a history of the United States, covering the latter half of the twentieth century. Several names are included, such as John Fitzgerald Kennedy, Richard Nixon, Ronald Reagan, and Bill Clinton. Some of the events are listed there as well, including words like Vietnam, the Sexual Revolution, the Berlin Wall, and Hope, Arkansas. But conspicuously missing are other words like Marilyn Monroe, Watergate, Iran/Contra Affair, or Monica Lewinski. In essence, it would not take the modern reader long to discover that they were reading an "antiseptic" or cleaned-up version of the historical period of the latter half of the twentieth century. This is one way of considering the books of 1 and 2 Chronicles. Missing are the indiscretions of David and many of the indiscretions of Solomon as well. We know of these darker days of the reigns of David and Solomon from the earlier books of Samuel and Kings, but they are notably missing in the work of Chronicles.

Like the books of Samuel and Kings, Chronicles is believed to have originally been written as a single book. The first written evidence of it being in two parts is found in the Septuagint. Clyde Francisco suggests that two books were necessary since vowels were added in the Greek translation. In the earlier Hebrew text the vowels, when used, are placed primarily beneath and between the consonants. The Greek text adds separate characters for each vowel, in effect doubling an existing written text.[1] The Hebrew title for the book of Chronicles is *Dibre Hayamim*, loosely translated, "the events or words of the days." The title used in the Septuagint is the Greek word *Paraleipomena*, or "things omitted." Our English title for this work is derived from the Latin Vulgate translated by Jerome around the fourth century CE with the title "A Chronicle of the Whole Divine History."

Second Chronicles is the last book of the Hebrew canon. The end of 2 Chronicles speaks of the Persian king Cyrus allowing the exiles to return in order to rebuild the temple in Jerusalem. There has been much speculation among scholars concerning the issue of authorship of both Chronicles and Ezra/Nehemiah. Scholarship still remains divided, with some scholars affirming a mutual author for Chronicles and at least Ezra, and others who see different authors for each of these major writings of the postexilic period. In our English Protestant canons, Chronicles and Ezra/Nehemiah remain together as part of a section loosely dubbed as part of the "historical" section of the Old Testament. In the Hebrew canon, however, the order is reversed, placing Ezra/Nehemiah before the book of Chronicles, concluding the *Ketuvim*, or Writings.

The author of the book of Chronicles is often referred to as the Chronicler. Using the historical framework already in place in the books of Samuel and Kings, the author of Chronicles retells the story of Israel, emphasizing a call to affirmation of faith in the God of Israel in the postexilic period. Throughout the books of 1 and 2 Chronicles, the past is interpreted through a theological lens of relevancy for the late fifth and early fourth centuries BCE. In 1 Chronicles 1–9 the history of Israel, beginning with Adam and continuing through Saul, is offered in the form of an extended genealogy. First Chronicles 10–29 details the history of David's reign as king of Israel. Second Chronicles 1–9 outlines the history of Solomon's reign as king of Israel. Second Chronicles 10:1–36:21 provides a detailed overview of the history of the kingdom of Judah during the time of the divided kingdom through the time of return from exile. The historical details of the northern kingdom are completely ignored in Chronicles. When Chronicles refers to Israel, it is referring to Israel as a general name describing Judah, not to the name used of the northern tribes during the time of schism between 922 and 722 BCE. Finally, 2 Chronicles 36:22-23 serves as a historical appendix, introducing the reader to the person of Ezra.

The purpose of the book of Chronicles is to provide a positive view of Israel's past and to express hope for the future beyond the postexilic period. Three dominant theological themes appear in the work of Chronicles. The first theme revolves around the centrality of worship, focusing on the use of the temple in the life of the nation. The author of Chronicles emphasizes the need to connect the worship of his or her day to the ancient practice of worship witnessed with the first temple, which was constructed under the watchful eye of Solomon. It is not too strong to say that the favorite hymn of the author of Chronicles may have been "Give Me That Old-Time Religion." This emphasis on the temple and worship was more than just a concern for proper religious practice. This emphasis helped to provide a national identity for the members of the nation of Israel who had now returned from exile.

A second theological theme expressed in Chronicles is the importance of the Davidic monarchy. In the eyes of the writer/editor of Chronicles, David could do no wrong. David is extolled as the "ideal" leader as both king and leader of worship. On the one hand David is the ideal king. On the other hand David is also the "patron saint" of worship. The stories of David's military victories and slaying of giants are minimized in favor of David's act of writing hymns and his desire to build the temple in Jerusalem. In crafting this historiography of David, the author of Chronicles intentionally omits any story that would serve to damage David's reputation. Absent in Chronicles are the stories of David and Bathsheba, the rebuke by Nathan the prophet, or Absalom's revolt against King David.

A revival of retribution theology is the third major theological theme witnessed in the book of Chronicles. Taking its cue from the books of Samuel and Kings, Chronicles emphasizes that the welfare of Israel is dependent upon the faithfulness of her leaders and people. If they are good, God will bless them, but if they turn from God and break the covenant with God, then God will once again bring punishment upon the people. A bright future awaits the people of Israel, but only if they will turn from their sin and commit themselves to keeping the Mosaic Law and the covenant God has made with God's people.

Unfortunately, Chronicles has often been relegated to the pages of obscurity in the Old Testament. It reflects an "antiseptic" description of the lives of David and Solomon, and it completely dismisses anything to do with the northern kingdom during the schism between Israel and Judah. There is still much rich treasure for the student who is willing to dig deep in the pages of Chronicles. There are bits and pieces of information that are not found anywhere else in the Old Testament and prove helpful in "filling in the gaps" when reading the Old Testament story. I must plead guilty to often overlooking the wealth of information in this book. In my introductory Old Testament classes at the undergraduate or graduate levels, I often leave the study of Chronicles off of the syllabus as a matter of choosing to save time. Much of the information is already available in Samuel and Kings, so I have often chosen to simply bypass the words in these pages. Throughout my thirty-plus years of serving as a full-time, part-time, bivocational, or interim pastor, I have often also ignored preaching from this book as well. I urge you to join me in rediscovering this book and allowing this part of God's word to bring its light once again into our hearts and mind.

The Texts of 1 Chronicles

An Overview of the Beginnings: Adam to Saul, 1–9

A few years ago I spoke to our local genealogical society. I had never been to a meeting before, so I really didn't know what to expect. They had asked me to discuss some of the nuances of the genealogies of the Old Testament. It was an interesting

1 & 2 CHRONICLES

evening, and I could tell that these people were really intrigued by the nexus of names, families, and backgrounds of the individuals located in various genealogical records in the biblical texts. These people would love 1 Chronicles 1–9. The introduction to the two-volume work of 1 and 2 Chronicles is one big list of names, beginning with Adam, branching through Noah, Abraham, the various heads of each tribe, the Levites and temple musicians, and adding the specific descendants of David, keeping with the author's fascination with everything related to David in the postexilic period.

Many of us are guilty of simply skipping through the lists when we encounter them throughout the pages of the Old Testament. These genealogies have an important place in the life of the Scripture, though. They are pivotal in maintaining the purity of Israel in the postexilic community. National identity and purity are important themes throughout the pages of Chronicles, Ezra, and Nehemiah. John Hayes wrote, "A Jew could no longer claim to be a Jew on the basis of membership in an independent political entity. His Jewishness was expressed in worship of Yahweh, his participation in the Temple cult, and his obedience to the Torah. The great interest in genealogical lists, as in the Priestly code, 1 Chronicles 1–9, and throughout Ezra and Nehemiah, must be seen against this backdrop."[2] The Levites and other temple personnel found these genealogies helpful in providing authority for their service as priests and singers in the temple and the leading of worship. First Chronicles 1–9 also provides a genealogical lifeline between the postexilic community and the promise to Abraham. The postexilic community is a continuation of the promise God made to Abraham in the book of Genesis.

First Chronicles 1 focuses on the genealogies of the primeval history and the patriarchal period. These names apparently come directly from the book of Genesis. One notable absence is the name Cain, who is omitted by the author of Chronicles. The author of Chronicles also lists Isaac before Ishmael, reversing the order as found in Genesis. Like Genesis 36, which provides a list of Edomite kings, 1 Chronicles 1:34-37 includes a brief genealogy of the

Edomites, who are the descendants of Esau. First Chronicles 2 provides a list of descendants from the house of Jacob, who is identified only as Israel in Chronicles. The ancestry of David is included in 2:9-17. First Chronicles 3 is devoted entirely to the lineages of David and Solomon. First Chronicles 3:1-9 provides the most complete list of David's progeny in the Hebrew Bible.

Bruce Wilkinson made 1 Chronicles 4:10 famous with his book *The Prayer of Jabez: Breaking Through to the Blessed Life*. First Chronicles 4:10 reads, "Jabez called on the God of Israel, saying, 'Oh that you would bless me and enlarge my border, and that your hand might be with me, and that you would keep me from hurt and harm!'" Clyde Francisco commented on this verse a quarter century before the verse became widely popular among Christians in North America: "Admittedly the prayer was an immature one, for Jabez asked to be spared pain at the expense of the suffering of people whom he would replace."**3** The name Jabez is derived from a Hebrew word for pain, *Jozeb*. The point of the naming of Jabez demonstrates that there is great power in the practice of prayer. God can bring great outcomes even from painful situations. As Francisco reminds us, long before the prayer of Jabez reached its height of popularity, we must be careful how we pray. Selfish prayers for our own well-being may be popular among many, but true prayer calls upon God to deliver us even from the most painful circumstances, not that we should pray to be afforded lives of luxury.

The genealogical lists in the Old Testament provide a treasury for rich discovery for those willing to invest themselves into these words and pages. First Chronicles 5–9 records additional names of the heads of the families of the various tribes of Israel, a list of temple musicians and the inhabitants of Jerusalem at the time of the compiling of the book of Chronicles in 1 Chronicles 9. The careful reader will notice the similarities between 1 Chronicles 9 and Nehemiah 11, detailing the inhabitants who have returned from captivity.

1 & 2 Chronicles

A Glimpse of David's Reign, 10-29

The various genealogies in 1 Chronicles 1-9 have now brought the reader to the beginning of Israel's history—at least the only history the author is concerned about. The author of Chronicles is not interested in cataloging the exploits of all the kings of Israel and Judah, leaving this task to the author of Samuel and Kings, sometimes referred to as the Deuteronomistic historian. In Chronicles the beginning genealogy has given the reader a historical overview of the family heads of Israel through the postexilic community. Beginning in chapter 10, the author of Chronicles introduces us to the historical period he is most concerned about—the reign of King David. The ending of Saul's life is the theme of 1 Chronicles 10. The author emphatically alerts the reader that Saul was unfaithful to the desires of the God of Israel. In simpler terms, the unfaithful Saul is set up as the strawman to David as a virtuous king. Saul is bad; David is good. First Chronicles 10 records that Saul "and all his house died together" (v. 6). Other descendants of Saul who were not present at Mount Gilboa are mentioned in the genealogy of Saul in 1 Chronicles 9:39-40. The remaining Chronicles narrative, however, never mentions the difficulty David had in the first years of his being named king while contending with Saul's son Ishbaal (literally, *ish baal*, or man of Baal), who was reigning over the ten northern tribes with Saul's general Abner as the commander of his army. With Saul out of the picture, now David is able to assume the mantle of leadership as appointed to him by God through the anointing of Samuel, as described in 1 Samuel 16.

As one continues to read through the description of David's reign through the eyes of the author of Chronicles, one begins to notice many more genealogies than were present in the account of David's reign as told in Samuel and Kings. Genealogies and lists dominate the texts of 1 Chronicles 10-29, describing everything from the mighty men of David in 11:20-47 to the divisions of priests in chapters 23 and 24. First Chronicles 11 and 12 outline David's coming of age as the king of Israel. In 12:23-40 David is finally proclaimed king over all twelve tribes of Israel.

The moving of the ark of the covenant from Kiriath-jearim to Jerusalem is the centerpiece of 1 Chronicles 13–16. In 2 Samuel 6:12-19 the reader is offered a picture of King David wearing only a linen undergarment of sorts and dancing before the ark during its entry into Jerusalem. His wife Michal is embarrassed by her husband's actions, and words are exchanged between the two after the fact. The processional of the ark is described in fuller detail in the Chronicles text. It also describes David as fully clothed in this account. First Chronicles 15:27 states, "David was clothed with a robe of fine linen, as also were all the Levites who were carrying the ark, and the singers, and Chenaniah the leader of the music of the singers; and David wore a linen ephod." Francisco speculates that Michal becomes incensed because David's robe may have flown open at some point and offers this description as complementary to the Samuel description.[4] As previously mentioned, this text serves as a classic example of the many ways the author of Chronicles "cleans up" the story of David. The reader is treated to a selection of psalms of thanksgiving for the safe delivery of the ark into Jerusalem in 1 Chronicles 16:8-36. This psalm includes excerpts from Psalms 105:1-15, 96:1-13, and 106:1, 47-48.

David's kingdom and future lineage are solidified in 1 Chronicles 17–20. The Davidic dynasty, built upon 2 Samuel 7, is an idea that states a Davidic heir would always remain as the king of Israel. First Chronicles 17 describes this event through the words of Nathan the prophet. The remaining chapters of 1 Chronicles 18–20 recount many of David's great victories over Israel's warring neighbors, especially the Philistines, who had become such a troublesome threat during the later period of the Judges. In 1 Chronicles 20:1-3 the author of Chronicles begins this story just as the story of David and Bathsheba is recounted in 2 Samuel 11:1: "In the spring of the year, the time when kings go out to battle." The author of Chronicles, however, unlike his Deuteronomistic counterpart, does not share the story of David and his tryst with Bathsheba. In 1 Chronicles 20:5 the author of Chronicles cleans up another earlier issue that is problematic in the Hebrew texts. The Hebrew text literally states in 1 Samuel 17:7 that Elhanan slew Goliath. The author in Chronicles once again comes to the rescue, correcting what can be seen as an obvious problem in the Samuel text. Chronicles states that Elhanan slew Lahmi, the brother of Goliath.

First Chronicles 21, in conjunction with 2 Samuel 24, has proven to be one of those conundrums that has hounded biblical scholars over the ages. These passages describe David numbering the men of fighting age in Israel. The heart of the problem centers upon the source of instruction given for the taking of the census of men. Second Samuel 24:1 records, "Again the anger of the LORD was kindled against Israel, and he incited David against them, saying, 'Go, count the people of Israel and Judah.'" As divine punishment, Gad the prophet comes to David and offers three choices placed before him by God. David can take three years of famine, three months of fleeing from his enemies, or three days of plague in the land. God sent a plague upon the land, and 70,000 people perished. The author of Chronicles, as he has proven himself prone to do, attempts at "cleaning up" this text by taking the onus off of God and placing it upon Satan. First Chronicles 21:1 states, "Satan stood up against Israel, and incited David to count the people of Israel." The author of Chronicles correctly perceives that if God had instructed David to number the men, then how could David be blamed? And why would God be so harsh for actions that God had set in motion? The author attributes the incident to Satan. This is the only time the word "Satan," from the Hebrew *Satan*, appears in the Old Testament as a proper name without the definite article. Satan is also portrayed as a tempter who lures David to sin before God by numbering the fighting men, therefore not trusting solely in God's provision. The word *hasatan*, or "the satan," meaning "adversary" or "accuser," does appear with the definite article in Job 1:6, 2:1, and Zechariah 3:1-2. This picture of Satan in Chronicles stands more closely related to the picture of Satan presented in the New Testament. Thus, in keeping with the theme of

Chronicles as maintaining a pristine picture of David, Satan is blamed for David's misdeed.

David's preparations for the building of the temple are described in elaborate detail in 1 Chronicles 22–29. David passes along his plan and trust to his son Solomon. First Chronicles 22:8 reminds the reader of the reason David is not allowed to build the temple: there is too much blood on David's hands. The name "Solomon" is derived from the Hebrew word for peace or wholeness, *shalom*. Some scholars suggest that Solomon may have simply been a name given to him when he ascended to power as king. In 2 Samuel 12:24 Solomon is identified as Jedidiah, or "beloved of the Lord."[5] Unlike his father David, Solomon grew up in the royal palace and reigned during a time of relative peace. Indeed, the great accomplishments attributed to Solomon as a master builder, supporter of culture and literature, and the originator of the Wisdom tradition in Israel are all a result of the relative peace enjoyed by the nation of Israel during Solomon's reign. The concluding chapters of 1 Chronicles are filled with lists identifying the Levites, the temple singers, the gatekeepers, the treasurers, and the soldiers serving at that time. David is center stage one last time in 1 Chronicles 29 as a beautiful prayer is attributed to David in vv. 10-19. This prayer is immediately followed by the anointing of Solomon as king. Nowhere in the Chronicles narrative do we find the struggle for kingship between Solomon and Adonijah as recounted in 1 Kings 1.

The Texts of 2 Chronicles

Fondly Remembering Solomon's Reign, 1–9

The narrative discussing Solomon's reign as king in 2 Chronicles 1–9 is cast in the same positive light as the texts discussing David's reign. The blights of Solomon's reign found in 1 Kings 1–11 are missing. The author of 2 Chronicles 1 chooses to introduce the reader to the reign of Solomon by retelling the story of Solomon asking God for wisdom, as previously written in 1 Kings 3. When confronted with the concept of asking God for whatever he wished, Solomon simply asked for wisdom. The concept of wisdom in the ancient Near East is not simply having a high acumen or intelligence level; it is better defined as living rightly, which leads to success in life. Solomon asked God to help him live and reign rightly. The famous story of Solomon's discernment displayed in the story of the two prostitutes with one dead baby and one live baby, recorded in 1 Kings 3:16-28, is omitted by the author of Chronicles. Solomon's decision was to cut the live baby in half, with each half to be given to the two mothers, leading to the discovery of the real mother, who pleaded for her child's life. This story has always been close to my heart. Several years ago when a book I coedited was first released for publication, the cover of the book had a painting of this famous scene of the live baby being delivered before Solomon. This release came just days after my wife and I lost our third son, who died in his sleep in a church nursery.[6] Like the mother pleading for her child to live, my wife and I would have done almost anything to exchange places with our son. The author of Chronicles doesn't include this famous story, partly because the telling of the reign of Solomon focuses almost solely on Solomon's building of the temple. The construction of the temple, not the mundane details of Solomon's reign, is the crux of the author's concern.

The years of Solomon's reign are elevated almost to sainthood status in 2 Chronicles 9:22-31. As the builder of the temple, Solomon is remembered throughout the Chronicles narrative without the misgivings that resonate in 1 Kings 11:1-13, which speaks of Solomon also building temples for his foreign wives and allowing altars to be placed throughout Israel to these foreign gods. Also, the consistent theme of putting away foreign wives, so prominent throughout the books of Ezra and Nehemiah, is never mentioned regarding Solomon with his 700 wives and 300 concubines. In contrast to the summation of Solomon's reign offered in the Kings account, Chronicles states in v. 22 that "King Solomon excelled all the kings of the earth in riches and in wisdom." The passage continues to detail the great riches gained under Solomon, including gold, silver, horses, and chariots. The actual truth of Solomon's life and reign probably lies somewhere between the optimistic picture described by Chronicles and the quasidastardly image provided by Kings.

A Brief Overview of the Kingdom of Judah, 10:1–36:21

The author of Chronicles diverges from the pattern established by the Deuteronomistic historian who edited or wrote the book of Kings and chooses to tell only the story of the southern kingdom, Judah. The author also consistently refers to Judah in 2 Chronicles 10–36 as Israel, which of course is the name traditionally associated with the northern kingdom. The wickedness of many of the kings during this time of a divided kingdom is highlighted, providing a rationale for the eventual destruction of Solomon's temple along with the years of exile endured by so many of the people. The author also highlights the accomplishments of the kings of Judah, who are credited for trying to lead in national spiritual reforms. The reigns of Jehoshaphat (19–21), Hezekiah (29–32), and Josiah (34–35) are all described in thankful terms as reformers who pointed the nation of Israel back to her true purpose and calling.

Along with the vaulted recognition given to these reformers, the author of Chronicles also includes images of restoration for kings who were given up as wicked in the picture offered of them in the book of Kings. One such example is Manasseh, who is seen as the most wicked king of Judah's history and is repeatedly castigated in the book of Kings as a wicked king (see 2 Kgs 21:1-18). Manasseh is also portrayed as a wicked king in Chronicles, but the author includes in 2 Chronicles 33:10-17 a story of Manasseh's change of heart when he was captured by the Assyrians. His prayer is answered by God, and his kingdom is restored, but the people did not follow his lead. The account in 2 Kings 21 does not mention any type of restoration or repentance on the part of Manasseh. One other key part of this story is the length of Manasseh's reign. Second Kings 21 says that Manasseh reigned for fifty-five years, making it the longest of any of the kings of Judah. The author of Chronicles may be working to redeem this apparent inconsistency with the application of retribution theology, which is so prevalent in the Old Testament. Retribution theology, also known as Deuteronomistic theology, says that if we are good, God blesses us, but if we are bad, then God punishes us. The repentance of Manasseh as described in Chronicles may just be another episode of the author "cleaning up" the inconsistency of the national theology of Israel. Or to say this another way, if retribution theology is real, then why does the God of Israel allow the most wicked king in the history of the southern kingdom to also have the longest tenure of any reigning king?

As an Old Testament professor at a private liberal arts university, I have always tried to temper any sense of judgment upon the reign of Manasseh with the historical realities surrounding the world in which he lived. While Manasseh did many detestable things, he also reigned during the height of the Assyrian Empire and was an active vassal to this empire. Manasseh's reign overlapped the reigns of the Assyrian kings Esarhaddon (681–669 BCE) and Ashurbanipal (669–626 BCE), two kings who reigned during the height of the empire. Esarhaddon led successful military campaigns into Egypt, reaching as far as Memphis in 671 BCE. Ashurbanipal was equally a strong king, who continued the conquest into Egypt, reaching Thebes in 663 BCE. Had Manasseh removed the Assyrian gods from the temple or acted in any manner that would have been perceived by the Assyrians as a move to independence, it probably would have brought about the immediate end of Israel at the hands of the Assyrians.

Second Chronicles 21:20 jumps out at the reader as a testament to the enduring poor reputation of King Jehoram of Judah: "He departed with no one's regret. They buried him in the city of David, but not in the tombs of the kings." There is an old saying that goes something like this: "Some people make people happy *wherever* they go. Some people make people happy *whenever* they go." It appears that Jehoram belonged to the latter group. What a sad ending for a king of Judah.

Verse 18 informs us that Jehoram had endured a brutally painful bowel illness that ultimately took his life. Then, following an illness lasting two years, he dies without fanfare or mourning. The parallel account in 2 Kings 8 does not mention the illness or the tidbit that Jehoram was not buried in the tombs of the kings. It seems that history had continued to be unkind to Jehoram. The further removed the reader becomes from the events of Jehoram's life and death, the more morose the retelling of the story becomes.

At Jehoram's death he left behind his wife, Athaliah, the granddaughter of Omri a northern king, and his son, Ahaziah, his youngest son, who succeeded Jehoram on the throne. The author of Chronicles portrays Ahaziah's reign as a short, evil one, following the ways of his mother, the daughter of Ahab, who is described as the most wicked king of Israel in the north. Ahaziah is killed by Jehu, who was busy leading a purge of the house of Omri in the northern kingdom of Israel. This assassination of the southern king of Judah by a northerner decimates the peace treaty that had held fast by the intermarriage of Athaliah and Jehoram as orchestrated by Omri. This is a significant development in the histories of both Israel and Judah. Upon the death of Jehoram and Ahaziah, Athaliah is left to reign as queen over the nation of Judah for six years. The author of Chronicles does not hide the personal disdain the preservers of Israel's history have for Athaliah. But her reign is very important nonetheless because for the only time in the ancient history of Israel or Judah, a woman is the primary head of these nations. In a patriarchal culture, recorded in a book written primarily for men by men, we have this historical record of an influential woman serving as the head of the nation of Judah. Second Chronicles 22:10-12 describes Athaliah's rise to power on the throne of Judah. Her death is recounted in 2 Chronicles 23:12-21 as she is put to the sword by the priest Jehoiada. Second Chronicles 23:21 states, "So all the people of the land rejoiced, and the city was quiet after Athaliah had been killed with the sword." Once again, the author of Chronicles is "cleaning up" the mess of the stories from Israel and Judah. The dynasty of Omri, which had reveled in the worship of the Canaanite god Baal, was ultimately ended, and nobler kings were allowed to lead, moving the nation to "purer" times.

Three kings serve as representatives for the author of Chronicles looking for heroes in presenting an idealized past that calls the people in the postexilic period to hope and restoration to the covenant between the God of Israel and God's people: Jehoshaphat, Hezekiah, and Josiah. This is only a representative list and does not exhaust the examples present throughout Chronicles.

The details of the reign of Jehoshaphat are outlined in 2 Chronicles 17–21. The name Jehoshaphat means "the Lord judges" in Hebrew. Jehoshaphat comes to power in Judah following the death of his father, Asa. His reign took place somewhere near the years of 870–846 BCE. The author of Chronicles speaks of Jehoshaphat in positive terms, saying he walked in the ways of his father, probably a reference to the dynasty of David, who is the first truly great king of Israel. He attempted to put away the altars to Baal worship and led religious reform throughout Judah. Second Chronicles 17:6 describes him as "courageous in the ways of the LORD." Jehoshaphat was seen as a great king and is portrayed as pointing the people back to the covenant between them and God. The specific details of his reform are described in 2 Chronicles 19:4-11. The description of Jehoshaphat is much more detailed in the Chronicles account than is found in the book of Kings. He is described as a great reformer in civil, military, and judicial life. An epitaph of Jehoshaphat is provided by the author of Chronicles in 2 Chronicles 20:31-37. This concluding biblical obituary to Jehoshaphat praises his faithfulness but also states that high places or pagan altars were not all removed from the land and that the reform did not take hold with the people.

Hezekiah reigned in Judah from 715 to 687 BCE. Details of his reign are expounded upon in 2 Chronicles 29–32. Hezekiah is often touted as one of the truly great kings of Judah's history. He was twenty-five years of age when he ascended to the throne. The account of Hezekiah in the book of Kings focuses upon giving an overview of his reign, including the building of the famous tunnel of Hezekiah, which brought water from the Gihon Spring outside the walls of the city of Jerusalem by digging a tunnel through over 1,700 feet of solid rock (2 Kgs 20:20). The tunnel still remains today, standing as part of the site of the old city of David, and is passable with a flashlight for pilgrims who don't mind getting their feet wet.

    The Kings account, along with the book of Isaiah, details Hezekiah's response to the Sennacherib crisis of 705–701 BCE. Sennacherib and the Assyrians besieged Jerusalem, holding the city and Hezekiah hostage inside the walls of the city. One account in Kings tells of Jerusalem's and Hezekiah's escape due to divine intervention in Sennacherib's camp (1 Kgs 19). A second account details how Sennacherib withdrew his siege of the city of Jerusalem only after Hezekiah stripped the temple treasury and paid the Assyrians a large sum of treasure (2 Kgs 18:13-16). The focus of Hezekiah's reign through the eyes of the author of Chronicles is Hezekiah as a great leader of Israel's worship. Second Chronicles 29 details Hezekiah leading in religious reform, faithfully removing foreign objects of worship from the temple. The next two chapters give careful detail concerning Hezekiah leading in a national celebration of the Passover and his further leading in worship. The author of Chronicles gives more voice to the reign of Hezekiah than to any other king save the reigns of David and Solomon. In the eyes of the author of Chronicles, Hezekiah is perhaps the greatest king of Israel's history who is not named David or Solomon. The aforementioned Sennacherib crisis is described in 2 Chronicles 32. The Chronicles account follows the "miraculous" event as described in 1 Kings 19 and does not mention the "payoff" version mentioned in the 2 Kings 18:13-16 and Assyrian accounts. The pride of Hezekiah is mentioned in 1 Chronicles 32, along with an illness that places Hezekiah at death's door. He is spared following his act of repentance. The author describes Hezekiah as a good king who is blessed by God and acquires great wealth for the land of Judah. Second Chronicles

1 & 2 Chronicles

32:30b offers a most flattering description of Hezekiah: "Hezekiah prospered in all his works." That is a far cry from the epithet used to describe Jehoram: "He departed with no one's regret."

Josiah was just eight years of age when he ascended to the throne following the death of Amon, Manasseh's son. The approximate dates of Josiah's reign are 640–609 BCE. The brief overview of Josiah's reign appears in 2 Chronicles 34–35 and is paralleled in 2 Kings 22–23. These two accounts extol the leadership of Josiah for championing a national reform movement. Only Chronicles, however, discusses the ownership of the people for this movement as partners with Josiah. During the renovation of the temple, a law book is discovered. The temple officials and priests are unable to adequately authenticate this discovery. The book is brought before Huldah, a female prophet, who authenticates the book as a word from God and delivers a sobering message to Judah of coming disaster. The text credits Josiah for responding to this message as he leads in a period of reform and covenant renewal.

Three pillars formed the basis of Josiah's reform. First, the temple was cleared of all pagan symbols of worship. Second, foreign forms of worship that had been part of Israel's culture dating back to the time of Solomon were also outlawed. Finally, the worship of the God of Israel was once again centralized. These three primary reforms have led some scholars to theorize that what Josiah actually found was at least a portion of the book of Deuteronomy, particularly the Deuteronomic Code located in Deuteronomy 12–26, since these three elements of the reform are highlighted in this portion of Deuteronomy. One idea suggests that this early form of Deuteronomy was written in the north and brought to Jerusalem just before the fall of Samaria in 722 BCE. The idea continues that the book was stored in the temple for safekeeping and lay dormant until it was literally brought to light during the restoration of the temple by Josiah.7 Just as Hezekiah's reform led to a national celebration of the Passover, Josiah's reforms are also followed by a national commemoration of the Passover, as described in 2 Chronicles 35. Josiah dies in battle with Pharaoh Necho at a battle near Megiddo in 609 BCE. The Egyptians were rallying to support the struggling Assyrian army who were fighting the growing power of Babylon. Pharaoh Necho was leading his armies to support Assyria when they were confronted by Josiah and the army from Judah. The Chronicles account claims that Necho was acting on behalf of a word he has received from God. Josiah is warned not to intervene, but he does, and the battle ends in defeat and the loss of Judah's beloved king.

At the death of Josiah, Judah falls under the direct supervision of the Egyptians. Necho arranges for Jehoiakim (609–597 BCE) to sit on the throne, forcing Judah to pay heavy tribute to the Egyptians. Josiah's death in 609 BCE signals the beginning of the end for the nation of Judah. The author of Chronicles quickly summarizes the remaining days of the southern kingdom in 2 Chronicles 36, and with this brief word the Hebrew canon is now complete. The author quickly summarizes in a few short verses the brief reigns of Jehoahaz, Jehoiakim, Jehoiachin, Zedekiah, the fall of Jerusalem, and concludes with the decree of Cyrus, which allowed the exiles to return. The final days of Judah are told in greater detail in 2 Kings 23–25.

Introduction to Ezra, 36:22-23

The final two verses of 2 Chronicles are often viewed as an introduction to the book of Ezra. It is significant, however, that Ezra/Nehemiah precedes the book of Chronicles in the Hebrew canon. The Chronicler states that Jeremiah is to be credited with the prophetic word, describing the work of Cyrus in allowing the exiles to return to their homeland. Perhaps the author has Isaiah in mind rather than Jeremiah while penning these words based on Isaiah 44:28 and 45:1. With the Cyrus decree the end of the exile has come. The early audience of this book was now faced with the reality of their own situation. The author has produced an overview of Israel's history, demonstrating how the nation of Israel had not lived up to their side of the covenant with God. Using David,

Solomon, and other faithful leaders as examples, the nation of Israel is once again called to renew themselves to the covenant of their fathers. With this renewal comes the possibility for a present and future hope.

Conclusion

Hope. Second Chronicles 7:14 is often quoted in evangelical revival and renewal services: "If my people who are called by my name humble themselves, pray, seek my face, and turn from their wicked ways, then I will hear from heaven, and will forgive their sin and heal their land." The author of Chronicles writes about this present and future hope. There is much irony in the book of Chronicles. These two books powerfully emphasize the wonder of David's reign as king and the importance of the Davidic dynasty, combined with the need for religious uniformity and purity. But this appeal is made during a period when there was no Davidic or Israelite king. It represents a hope that endured throughout the exilic and postexilic periods that one day Israel and the Davidic dynasty would return once again, establishing justice to the land of promise.

Being a product of my social environment, I grew up idolizing the Cleveland Indians and the Cleveland Browns. I still remember the "old-timers" speaking in hush tones of the great Larry Doby, Bob Feller, Herb Score, Lou Boudreau, Rocky Colavito, or Jim Brown, Lou Groza, and Paul Brown. But the players I personally remember were associated not with championships, but were rather players associated with coming up just short again and again. I grew up with names like Sudden Sam McDowell, Rico Carty, Frank Duffy, Jack Brohamer or Bernie Kosar, Brian Sipe, Leroy Kelly, and Paul Warfield. As I close this chapter on the works of 1 and 2 Chronicles, I am reminded of my own exile from professional sports championships based primarily on my place of birth, northern Ohio. The postexilic community, in a sense, is holding on to the heroes of their faith: David, Solomon, Hezekiah, and Josiah are all remembered for their great deeds of old. The historical facts of the postexilic community are that life was pretty hard for these people. They were still a people who were accountable to a foreign government with no living king. But there was hope. The Davidic lineage did continue, and the temple was restored with an active priesthood. Perhaps that is the greatest contribution of Chronicles. It offers hope in the midst of dire times—like the hapless Indians or Browns fans, who always seems to have a smile on their faces no matter how bad our teams may be. We can endure incredible loss and suffering as long as there is still hope.

For Further Reading

Ackroyd, Peter R. *Exile and Restoration.* The Old Testament Library. Philadelphia: Westminster Press, 1968.

Francisco, Clyde T. "1–2 Chronicles." *The Broadman Bible Commentary*, vol. 3. Nashville: Broadman Press, 1970.

Hayes, John H. *Introduction to the Bible.* Philadelphia: Westminster Press, 1971.

Japhet, Sara. *1 & 2 Chronicles.* The Old Testament Library. Louisville: Westminster John Knox Press, 1993.

Matthews, Victor H. and James C. Moyer. *The Old Testament: Text and Context.* Peabody MA: Hendrickson Publishers, 1997.

Soggin, J. Alberto. *Introduction to the Old Testament.* The Old Testament Library. Philadelphia: Westminster Press, 1989.

Notes

[1] Clyde T. Francisco, "1–2 Chronicles," in *The Broadman Bible Commentary*, vol. 3 (Nashville: Broadman Press, 1970) 297.

[2] John H. Hayes, *Introduction to the Bible* (Philadelphia: Westminster Press, 1971) 272.

[3] Francisco, "1–2 Chronicles," 312.

[4] Ibid., 334.

[5] Ibid., 347.

[6] For a longer description of this chapter in my life, please see David Crutchley and Gerald Borchert, eds., *Assaulted by Grief:*

Finding God in the Broken Places (Jefferson City TN: Mossy Creek Press, 2011).

[7]For a more complete discussion, please see Sara Japhet, *I & II Chronicles*, in The Old Testament Library (Louisville: Westminster John Knox Press, 1993) 1032–37.

Chapter 7

Ezra/Nehemiah

The time between the rededication of the second temple, circa 515 BCE, and the Maccabean revolt, circa 166 BCE, is surrounded by a mysterious shroud. There are historical documents from Israel's neighbors and the superpowers in these years, namely Persia and Greece. There remains, however, among biblical scholars, much debate concerning the events, the writings, and the reconstruction of definitive timelines and events during this period. Broadly speaking, a generalized timeline[1] is as follows:

515 BCE	Dedication of the Second Temple
486–465 BCE	Xerxes I, Persian King
465–423 BCE	Artaxerxes I, Persian King
458 BCE (?)	Ezra travels to Israel, bringing the Law of Moses from captivity
445 BCE	Nehemiah returns as governor (?) and oversees the rebuilding of the walls
404–358 BCE	Artaxerxes II, Persian King
398 BCE (?)	Ezra travels to Israel, bringing the Law of Moses from captivity
336–323 BCE	Alexander the Great, Greek King
166 BCE	Beginning of the Maccabean Revolt
164 BCE	Rededication of the Second Temple

As you may deduce from the question marks in the timeline above, there is much scholarly debate about the timeline of Ezra and Nehemiah among biblical scholars. Ezra precedes Nehemiah in the biblical texts, yet the scholarly debate continues concerning who arrived in Jerusalem first. Another scholarly debate centers on the issue of a title for Nehemiah. Was he really the governor of Judah, or was he simply an important official from the Persian court, selected with a specific purpose to return to Jerusalem?

It is a general consensus that the biblical books of Ezra and Nehemiah were originally one book in the Hebrew Bible. Some believe they were part of a specific collection, along with the book of Chronicles. In the third century CE Origen described this solitary volume as two separate works. Around 400 CE Jerome gave the name "Nehemiah" to the second portion of the narrative.[2]

Ezra and Nehemiah can be divided into two major sections. Ezra 1–6 tells the story of the postexilic restoration, beginning with the Edict of Cyrus down to the rededication of the second temple. Ezra 7–10, along with Nehemiah 1–13, relates the story of the return of the exiles to Jerusalem and the rebuilding of the walls of Jerusalem, punctuated by the national call for purification of Jewish religion and culture. Several sources have been identified throughout Ezra and Nehemiah. The Cyrus edict is preserved in Ezra 1:2-4, recorded in Hebrew. A second edict, written in Aramaic, is found in Ezra 4:8–6:18 and 7:12-26. The memoirs of Nehemiah represent another collection of source materials for this writing. The memoirs of Nehemiah are located in Nehemiah 1–7, 10, 12:17-43, and 13. These memoirs detail two specific official missions for Nehemiah, the most notable being the rebuilding of the walls. The memoirs of Ezra are the most controversial of the possible sources with some scholars doubting the existence of this pre-Ezra/Nehemiah source. Scholars such as Alberto Soggin point to Ezra 7–10 and Nehemiah 8 as examples of the Ezra memoirs.[3] A final source is the many lists found throughout the writings of Ezra and

Nehemiah. These lists include genealogies, signatories for covenant agreements, and a list of returnees from the exile.

It does appear from the texts of Ezra and Nehemiah that the two were not contemporaries for three primary reasons. Neither one mentions the other or appears to be part of the mission described by both, except for a questionable appearance of the two together mentioned in Nehemiah 8. Also, Nehemiah 3:1 states that Eliashib was the high priest during the time of Nehemiah. Eliashib's grandson, Jehohanan, was the high priest during the time of Ezra, as reported in Nehemiah 12. Finally, when Nehemiah returned to Jerusalem, he discovered Jerusalem was in ruins (Neh 2:17; 7:4). Ezra 9:4 and 10:1 describe Ezra coming to a city that was alive with activity upon his arrival.

Ezra and Nehemiah are great writings that can bring forth courage in the face of adversity, purity in the midst of temptation, and hope from the depths of discouragement. Ezra and Nehemiah are best known as the courier of the Law of Moses and the great builder of the wall of Jerusalem, respectively. Three primary characters dominate these texts. Zerubbabel, who was prominently featured in Haggai and Zechariah, is the main character in Ezra 1–6. He is called the governor of Judah and oversees the reconstruction of the temple under the reign of Darius I of Persia. He was a royal prince and descendant of King Jehoiachin, who was the first king of Judah taken into Babylonian captivity, according to 1 Chronicles 3:16-20. Ezra implies Zerubbabel was perceived as a threat and removed from leadership by the Persians before the completion of the temple, as stated in Ezra 6:14-15. The second primary character is Nehemiah, who is perhaps the main character of the period of restoration. He came to Jerusalem approximately seventy years after the rededication of the second temple with the charge to rebuild the walls of Jerusalem from Artaxerxes I of Persia. In spite of fierce opposition by the Samaritan community, Nehemiah is able to complete the task of rebuilding the walls of Jerusalem. Ezra is the third major character in these two books. He is sometimes called the second Moses, as he returns to Jerusalem with copies of the Law. Ezra's mission is described as receiving his commission from Artaxerxes II to lead a group of Jews back to Jerusalem with a caravan of gifts for the temple. He also sets out to establish the Jewish Torah as the legitimate law for the Israelite community.

Ezra and Nehemiah share the same religious emphases found sprinkled throughout the pages of 1 and 2 Chronicles. There is an emphasis on religious purity. The people of Israel must be kept pure from religious contamination. There is an emphasis on worship in the temple. David is viewed as the great patron saint of the worship of Israel. A theology of Zion dominates the theological perspective of the writers. Much like the theology of retribution demonstrated repeatedly in Joshua through Kings, there is also an emphasis on the immediate retribution for all slanders against the God of Israel. The sovereignty of God over all of history is also affirmed in Ezra and Nehemiah. Finally, like the writing of 1 and 2 Chronicles, the text takes the reader through a journey, vacillating between a sense of realized eschatology, salvation has come, and the reality that the hope is to be long awaited in some future hope.

The Texts of Ezra/Nehemiah

Return of the Exiles under Zerubbabel, Ezra 1:1–6:22

Ezra 1–6 focuses on the manner in which the God of Israel opened the door for the people who were in exile in Babylon, but are now under Persian rule, to be allowed to return to their sacred land. Ezra 1:1 references "the first year of King Cyrus," most likely referring to the first year of Cyrus's conquering the Babylonian Empire (539/538 BCE) and not to the first year of his reign, which took place in 559 BCE. The author then turns the attention of the reader to the events of the return as fulfillment of the preexilic prophet Jeremiah, who foretold of the return of a remnant from exile throughout his prophetic writing (two such examples include Jer 25:11-12 and 29:10-14).

The decree of Cyrus is recorded in Ezra 1:2-4, granting the returning exiles the right to rebuild the temple in Jerusalem. This version is written in Hebrew. A later version of this decree is also recorded later in Ezra 6:3-5, but is written in Aramaic. It is also recorded in 2 Chronicles 36:22-23. Emmett Willard Hamrick suggests the Ezra 1 and 2 Chronicles 36 versions represent an oral transmission of the decree delivered to the inhabitants of Jerusalem while the Ezra 6 version represents the formal written proclamation.[4] The author of Ezra leaves little doubt that the God of Israel is responsible for the return of the exiles to Palestine. God has also chosen to use Cyrus as God's agent in this process. This decree is not unique in Cyrus's reign. Several inscriptions ascribed to Cyrus's reign portray him as allowing several people groups who had been subjugated under Babylon rule to rebuild their localized temples and restore their national religion.

Ezra 1:5 to Ezra 2:70 describes the return from captivity, complete with lists containing articles taken from the temple during the siege of Nebuchadnezzar that are now to be returned to be used in the rebuilt temple. Ezra 2:1-70 provides an extensive list of the male heads of families who have returned from captivity.

Ezra 3 details the rebuilding of Israel's worship structure. The first step is the rebuilding of the altar, described in 3:1-7. The rebuilding of the altar also brought about the restored place of the priesthood in Israel. Their first act of collective worship mentioned in the text is the celebration of the Festival of Booths, or *Sukkoth*, a fall harvest festival, as prescribed in Leviticus 23:34. Next comes the founding of the second temple, described in Ezra 3:8-13. This receives a mixed response as those who remembered the previous temple begin to weep. This weeping is perhaps a mixture of joy and sadness as they recalled what once was and the lost years that intervened between the destruction of the temple and its rebuilding following the exile.

Ezra 4–6 tells of the opposition and support surrounding the rebuilding of the temple. Verses 1-3 note that the "adversaries of Judah" offered their aid in the rebuilding of the temple but were rebuffed by Zerubbabel. These people described as adversaries were not part of the exilic families who had returned from Babylonian captivity. Having been rebuked for their attempts to join the rebuilding, they appeal to the Persian king Artaxerxes I to aid in their efforts to thwart the building of the temple. Their efforts were initially successful until Darius I later intervened upon finding a copy of the earlier Cyrus edict, mentioned in Ezra 6:3-5, which allowed the temple construction to continue and be completed. Ezra 6:16-22 describes the dedication of the second temple and the ensuing celebration by the postexilic community. Ezra 6:22 adds a curious title to describe Darius I. He is alluded to in the passage as the king of Assyria. Some scholars simply discount any problem with this obvious anachronism by saying that Darius, as king of Persia, was king over all the land once part of the vast Assyrian Empire. But there may be more in play in this instance. There are several similar misspeaks throughout Ezra-Nehemiah, possibly pointing to a later editor or author being involved who was not particularly careful with the historical details of the story.

The Return of Ezra with the Law, Ezra 7:1–10:44

Ezra makes his initial appearance in the book of Ezra in Ezra 7:1-10. Observant readers will notice the large chronological gap between Ezra 6:22 and 7:1. As a reader we have just celebrated with the postexilic community the celebration of the completion of the second temple, and now we are at least 65 years later and perhaps over 115 years later, depending upon which Artaxerxes is intended in the text. As demonstrated previously in this chapter with the tentative timeline, Ezra's appearance in Jerusalem is dated to 458 if Artaxerxes I (465–423 BCE) is the preferred king or to 398 BCE if Artaxerxes II (404–358 BCE) is preferred. The author takes careful pains to establish Ezra's priestly credentials to the reader. Ezra is linked genealogically to both Aaron (7:5) and Zadok (7:2), thus bridging the traditional priestly rift in earlier days. The author also introduces the reader to Ezra's scribal training as a well-regarded student and teacher of the Mosaic Law (7:6, 10).

Ezra 7:11-26 is written in Aramaic and contains a royal introduction of Ezra and his mission to Judah. The form of the text is a letter given by Artaxerxes to Ezra, bestowing upon him his blessing and detailing the king's allowance for others to join Ezra on this quest. Verse 14 makes another allusion to Ezra's close ties to the Mosaic Law by mentioning "the law of your God, which is in your hand." The letter also makes allowance for financial provisions for Ezra and his entourage. It almost appears to be a "blank check" according to v. 20. In 7:27 the text once again resumes in Hebrew, and the memoirs of Ezra begin.

Ezra 7:27 through Ezra 10 gives a first-person account from Ezra concerning the return to Jerusalem and Ezra's leadership in the efforts of national purification of the people of Israel. Ezra 9 and 10 comprise the heart of the matter for which Ezra is well known. It is relayed to Ezra that many of the men of Israel had taken wives from the surrounding areas outside the national bloodline of Israel. The text describes Ezra responding with a traditional rite of mourning or contrition. The prayer of Ezra before God concludes 9:6-15. Throughout this prayer Ezra confesses the national sins of his countrymen of following the detestable practices of other lands brought to them primarily through the activity of intermarriage. In the final chapter of Ezra, Ezra calls the nation together and leads in a national call to purification and extols the people to "put away" or divorce their foreign wives or spouses. Ezra 10:18-44 gives a rather detailed list of the men who had taken foreign wives.

Ezra 9–10 is a great example of a biblical text or story that has been used as a bully club to support one's own personal agenda. It pains me to confess that I, too, have been guilty of preaching a gospel other than the gospel of Jesus Christ, using this text as a platform. Very early in my ministry, I preached a sermon called "The Case of the Ignorant Generation" in a small rural Baptist church in Oklahoma. It was fairly well received and represented a common understanding of many members of our local Baptist church constituents across the South and Southwest. It isn't hard to guess that my message was slanted unfavorably toward "mixed marriages" in our land today. I have wept many times over the arrogance and lack of judgment I used in this early message. Many times I have had to go back and look at my early writings or sermons and "Christianize" them after reflecting, praying, and interpreting life through experience, inspiration, and further study of God's Word. I am glad that I only preached that message once, and now I have a new message from that sermon. It is no longer titled "The Case of the Ignorant Generation," but it is now titled "The Case of the Ignorant Young Preacher Boy." William Holladay suggests in his work *Long Ago God Spoke* that the book of Ruth was possibly written as a response to Ezra's initiative, asking a quiet question: "Excuse me, what about King David?"[5] Holladay proposes that Ruth is to be understood as answering Ezra's position with the story about the ancestry of David, arguably the most beloved king of Israel's history. The story of Ruth details that David's great-grandmother, Ruth, was actually a Moabitess. If Naomi and Boaz had followed the same theological reasoning offered in Ezra, then Israel would have been denied leadership from their most beloved king.

The heart of the matter in Ezra 9–10 really isn't about marriage at all. It is about the question "Who is the Lord of your life?" For Israel in Ezra's context, the people were admonished not to intermarry with the Canaanites and other nationalities outside of Israel for fear they would be led into idolatry and the worship of other gods and goddesses related to foreign religions. This issue closely relates to the misgivings recorded of King Solomon in 1 Kings 11:1-13, where Solomon has taken many foreign wives and has begun to build temples to many of these foreign gods and goddesses. The writer of the book of Kings does not reprimand Solomon for the number of wives taken, but rather that he has allowed the worship of foreign gods to become commonly practiced in Israel. The heart, therefore, of the message in Ezra 9–10 is about keeping one's heart pure before God instead of following the false religions of our world. Moses also takes a Cushite wife, as told in Number 12, and is immediately castigated by Aaron and Miriam for doing so. They are countermanded by God for their stance and ordered by God to leave Moses alone. Recent world history has reminded us of the dangers of trumping a pure race or nationality over treating all people with dignity and respect. The point we should take from Ezra is that we are to keep ourselves from false worship and the idolatry that so permeates our world today, especially in the practice of Christianity in America in the twenty-first century.

Nehemiah's Return and the Building of the Wall, Nehemiah 1:1–6:19

Nehemiah 1:1-11 introduces the reader to the memoirs of Nehemiah. The opening line, "The words of Nehemiah son of Hacaliah," serves as the title or superscription to the text and alerts the reader from the beginning that the words they are reading have been edited in order to place the story in a historical context. Verse 1b provides more historical context by giving a dating formula of "in the twentieth year, while I was in Susa the capital." The twentieth year is believed to be the twentieth year of the reign of Artaxerxes I, establishing the time period of Nehemiah at 445/444 BCE. Artaxerxes is mentioned by name in Nehemiah 2:1, unlike in Ezra, where there is much debate over the matter of which Artaxerxes, I or II? Artaxerxes I can be safely assumed in Nehemiah due to a collaborating document from the Elephantine Jewish community in Egypt in the late fifth century, which speaks of a Jehohanan serving as high priest in Jerusalem and the sons of Sanballat serving as authorities in northern Palestine. Nehemiah was a contemporary of both Sanballat and Jehohanan's grandfather, Eliashib. Thus, since the Elephantine document predates the time of Artaxerxes II, the Artaxerxes associated with Nehemiah must be Artaxerxes I.[6] Nehemiah is described in v. 11 as a cupbearer to the king. Verse 1 says that Nehemiah was physically at Susa, described as the capital in the text. Persian texts demonstrate that Susa was the winter residence of the Persian kings.

In Nehemiah, God places a burden upon the heart of Nehemiah. In a conversation with Hanani and other men who had ventured from Jerusalem, Nehemiah learns of the awful conditions the people of Israel who had returned from captivity were living in. Nehemiah 1:3 describes the conditions in Jerusalem as those of devastation and loss. Nehemiah responds by sitting and weeping. The report elicited an emotional response from Nehemiah. Verse 4 gives a vivid description of the practice of mourning in the mid-fifth century BCE. Part of this mourning was an unspecified period of praying and fasting. In vv. 5-11 Nehemiah pleads for the people of Israel before God. Nehemiah confesses the sin that the people of Israel have committed is namely not keeping the covenant made between the people and God. Nehemiah cries out to God to hear his prayer and to respond to the desperate situation facing the people in Jerusalem. As one reads the text through fresh eyes, one can wonder what Nehemiah knew and when, concerning his response that God had chosen him to return to Jerusalem in order to lead in the rebuilding of its walls.

In Nehemiah 2, Nehemiah is confronted by Artaxerxes I concerning his melancholy demeanor. Nehemiah explains to the king that he is discouraged because he has learned of the hardships facing those living in his ancestral home. As many as three months have transpired since Nehemiah learned of these conditions from Hanani at Susa. Verse 2 explains that Nehemiah was anxious about the best way to approach the king with his problem. Artaxerxes asks Nehemiah specifically what he wanted. Nehemiah puts forth his request to return to Jerusalem and lead in rebuilding the city. Ezra 4:8-23 relates that the king had put a halt to rebuilding efforts under the leadership of Rehum and Shimshei; thus, Nehemiah's request is asking for a reversal of the king's earlier decision. The king agrees to Nehemiah's request, granting supplies and a military escort and acquiring a mutually agreed time for Nehemiah to return to his service. Nehemiah 5:14 tells us that Nehemiah's first term of service in Judah lasts twelve years.

After an initial personal inspection of the conditions of the city, Nehemiah calls upon the people to begin to rebuild the walls of Jerusalem. It is significant that Nehemiah uses personal pronouns concerning the construction plans. He uses words like "us" and "we" when describing his goal of building up the infrastructure of Jerusalem. Nehemiah calls for a cooperative effort in rebuilding the walls. There are many leadership styles present in our world, and each one has its own strengths and weaknesses. The collaborative style may be harder to implement initially, and it takes great effort to maintain, but the results are protected against the dangers found in following a singular personality who makes all the decisions for a group. When people invest in the vision and purpose modeled by a careful leader, the results have a greater chance of being timeless rather than temporary. Nehemiah shares that his authority came from two distinct sources in v. 18: the "hand of my God," and "the words that the king had spoken to me." Verses 10, 19, and 20 state that from the very beginning of his arrival, Nehemiah is faced with opposition primarily from Sanballat, Tobiah, and Geshem. Sanballat is identified as a Samaritan, a descendant of the intermingling of people groups in northern Palestine who were not part of the exilic experience in Babylon or, later, Persia. It was not enough for Nehemiah to find a daunting task in the conditions of the devastated city of Jerusalem, but now on top of the immediate task, Nehemiah faces the challenge of public opposition. It doesn't matter who you are or how talented you may be in the art of leadership; whenever you accept a place of leadership, you have also accepted the open criticism and often public opposition that surrounds every position of service. Verse 20 responds to the critics of his plan and mission with my paraphrase of two words: "Keep working." Nehemiah responds with humility, stating that God will give them success. If leaders are not careful, one can spend too much time worrying about the opposition or criticism and neglect the task at hand. Nehemiah does not make this mistake!

Nehemiah 3 describes the various individuals and groups who worked together to complete the construction on the wall. There were thirty-nine men named, with six being Levites or priests. There were six companies of builders recognized only by the town they represented: Jericho, Tekoa, Hassenaah, Gibeon, Mispah, and Zanoah. Verse 12 adds that the daughters of Shallum also participated in the construction. The people of

Jerusalem and her surrounding villages came together to work on the walls. Each group worked on a section of the wall assigned to them. Each worked on its appointed task. Organizations, groups, and local churches function so much better when everyone does a little bit to help. Unfortunately, too many times, a small percentage engages in most of the efforts. Sometimes this is done because of the unwillingness of others, but often it comes about because a few people want to control what is being done in the organization. When each of us participates in our specified task, we have little time for gossip, in-fighting, or general unrest. A wise leader keeps the people of an organization busy working toward the mission or goal of the organization. Notice that Nehemiah as leader is not mentioned a single time in chapter 3, though a different Nehemiah is mentioned in v. 16.

The threat from ongoing opposition continues in Nehemiah 4. Sanballat and Tobiah openly criticize the work of Nehemiah and the people. As is usually the case, the ones who are criticizing are not the ones actually doing the work. The workers are too busy with the task at hand. Nehemiah 4:1-3 relays some of the taunts the opponents were lobbing against the work party. At first glance the threats are only verbal, but as one reads throughout the chapter, the threats moved from improper thoughts, to improper words, and presumably were heading to improper actions. In vv. 4-9 Nehemiah responds quickly to the presumed threat. In vv. 4-5 we immediately see a prayer offered up on behalf of the people. This prayer is rather harsh in its tone, as it is filled with fear and anger. But in the midst of threat, what did Nehemiah and the people do? They just kept working, according to v. 6. A negative spirit is contagious and problematic. What started as "harmless" taunts is now festering into an apparent threat of physical violence. We should often guard our thoughts, and especially our words, very carefully. Ideas often give way to words, words can give power to sway others in our negativism, and collectively those words can lead to action.

In addition to the external threat found in chapter 4, Nehemiah and the workers face an equally real internal threat in 4:10-23. The walls were halfway completed, and the people were growing tired and discouraged. Discouragement often follows when a difficult task is undone and the "new" of the moment begins to wane. Verse 10 states that their strength was "failing." Nehemiah once again takes positive action toward this difficult issue, posting guards at selected places along the wall. Nehemiah also commands the people to build with one hand and to keep their swords ready with the other in v. 17. The image of the God of Israel as a divine warrior is once again revisited in Nehemiah 4:20: "Our God will fight for us." Nehemiah reminds the people that they are not alone in their struggle. God is able to deliver them from their enemies as God had done many times in the history of Israel. How often do God's people need to be constantly reminded of the resources, resilience, and the presence of God in the midst of life's battles and threats?

Yet another threat arose that worked against Nehemiah and the people rebuilding the wall of Jerusalem in Nehemiah 5. Economic hardship took its toll on the people of Jerusalem. Verses 1 and 2 indicate a shortage of food in the land. Verse 3 states that many people were forced into great debt to pay for daily living expenses. Heavy taxation surfaces in v. 4 as a cause of burden upon the people. Doesn't this seem vaguely familiar in our twenty-first-century world? Two wars in two decades, economic inequity, corporate profit and greed, and an ever-increasing gap between the haves and have-nots continue to pull at the American people today. Nehemiah confesses that when the economic injustice was brought to his attention, he became very angry. There are few issues so divisive to a harmonious community than extreme disparity in personal wealth and income. Nehemiah faced a population reflecting desperation, exasperated because those causing the inequity were supposedly fellow countrymen. Verse 7 says that Nehemiah considered these things. He didn't fly off the handle; rather, he carefully thought through his next courses of action. Nehemiah went to the source of the problem. He called together the nobles and officials who were perpetuating the widening gap and held them accountable for practicing dishonest usury and placing their fellow countrymen into further debt. The leaders comply with Nehemiah's request to restore a sense of "fair" business practice among the people. Nehemiah explains in vv. 14-19 that he had served as governor for twelve years and did so by not adding to the financial burden of the people, forgoing the customary taxes levied to provide for the living expense of the governor. Economic realities take their toll on people and families. What is missing in Nehemiah 5? There is no mention at all of the continued work of rebuilding the wall. When the people are focused on the basic necessities of survival, it is difficult to focus on anything else.

Nehemiah 6 recounts Nehemiah and the people finishing the job of building the walls of Jerusalem. Though plagued by constant external threat, discouragement from within, and economic hardship, Nehemiah 6:15 says the wall was completed in fifty-two days. Josephus, writing in the first century CE, says the work was completed in two years and four months, but many scholars do not generally accept this later assessment.[7] Verse 16 reflects a wonderful thought: "And when all our enemies heard of it, all the nations around us were afraid and fell greatly in their own esteem; for they perceived that this work had been accomplished with the help of our God." Successfully following the call of God in our lives inspires others around us to take part in God's work in our world, and it also discourages the naysayers from intervening in the work that God is undertaking. The wall is completed. Hard work, discipline, much prayer, and perseverance have enabled the people to overcome all the obstacles that came their way.

The Renewal of the People, Nehemiah 7:1–13:3

Nehemiah 7 begins with further instructions for the keepers of the gates on the walls and then produces another list of persons who had returned from exile, similar to the list found in Ezra 2. Nehemiah 8 describes the only intersection between Ezra and Nehemiah throughout these two texts. Ezra is described as reading the Law of Moses before the people who are gathered in a massive assembly before the water gate. All the people stood before the reading of the Law of Moses. As Ezra read, the Levites instructed the people on the meaning of the words being read, probably translating the Hebrew into Aramaic, which was the language of the people. Their gathering concluded in the practice of commemorating the Feast of Booths, or *Sukkoth*, for seven days. As previously mentioned in the introduction to this chapter, the appearance of Ezra in the context of the narrative of Nehemiah seems oddly out of place.[8]

Nehemiah 9 finds the people of Israel confessing their sinfulness corporately before God. A list of those taking part in this renewed covenant ceremony is provided in chapter 10. Nehemiah 11 shows a list of new inhabitants who were selected by lot to come and populate the city of Jerusalem once again. One out of every ten persons was to relocate to Jerusalem.

The dedication of the wall of Jerusalem is recorded in Nehemiah 12:27-47. It was a grand event, featuring the Levites leading their priestly duties with musical celebration, rites of purification for themselves, the people, and the wall itself. Two large choirs are described as taking place in this ceremony and were positioned on top of the wall at specified places, along with the leaders of the community.

Nehemiah's Second Return, Nehemiah 13:4-31

The final words in Nehemiah record the return of Nehemiah to Jerusalem, where he finds the people guilty of desecrating the temple by allowing Tobiah to have quarters within the temple area. Apparently, the jubilation and ceremony recorded in Nehemiah 12 had little lasting effect on the overall spiritual condition of the people. The length of Nehemiah's absence from Jerusalem is unspecified, but it is apparently long enough that things began to decay dramatically from a standpoint of general immorality among the people. Nehemiah also discovers the people are guilty of desecrating the Sabbath by working on their own and conducting commerce as on any other day. Nehemiah further discovers that people were intermarrying with non-Israelites once again and calls the people to put away their sinful behaviors.

Conclusion

Ezra and Nehemiah are important additions to the biblical material from the standpoint of understanding religious history in a time period that is woefully lacking other existing written sources. These books are also very important for the reader in discovering what religious practices were like in Judah in the postexilic communities. Fierce adherence to the laws and practices set down from the time of Moses along with the desire to conduct worship like David, the patriarch of Israel's worship, are both centerpieces in the book of Ezra/Nehemiah. Though both Ezra and Nehemiah represent the shadow of the Persian Empire over Judah, they also both demonstrate a deep personal commitment to the spiritual and physical well-being of their own people, the Israelites.

For Further Reading

Ackroyd, Peter R. *Exile and Restoration.* The Old Testament Library. Philadelphia: Westminster Press, 1968.

Brown, Raymond. *The Message of Nehemiah.* The Bible Speaks Today. Leicester, England: InterVarsity Press, 1998.

Bright, John. *A History of Israel.* Philadelphia: Westminster Press, 1981.

Cate, Robert L. *An Introduction to the Old Testament and Its Study.* Nashville: Broadman Press, 1987.

Hamrick, Emmett Willard. "Ezra–Nehemiah." *The Broadman Bible Commentary*, vol. 3. Nashville: Broadman Press, 1970.

Hayes, John H. *Introduction to the Bible.* Philadelphia: Westminster Press, 1971.

Holladay, William L. *Long Ago God Spoke.* Minneapolis: Fortress Press, 1995.

Matthews, Victor H. and James C. Moyer. *The Old Testament: Text and Context*. Peabody MA: Hendrickson Publishers, 1997.

Soggin, J. Alberto. *Introduction to the Old Testament*. The Old Testament Library. Philadelphia: Westminster Press, 1989.

Williamson, H. G. M. *Ezra, Nehemiah*. Word Biblical Commentary, vol. 16. Waco: Word Books, 1985.

Notes

[1] Condensed from John H. Hayes, *Introduction to the Bible* (Philadelphia: Westminster Press, 1971) 270.

[2] Robert L. Cate, *An Introduction to the Old Testament and Its Study* (Nashville: Broadman Press, 1987).

[3] J. Alberto J. Soggin, *Introduction to the Old Testament*, The Old Testament Library (Philadelphia: Westminster Press, 1989) 491–92.

[4] Emmett Willard Hamrick, "Ezra-Nehemiah," in *The Broadman Bible Commentary*, vol. 3. (Nashville: Broadman Press, 1970) 432.

[5] William L. Holladay, *Long Ago God Spoke* (Minneapolis: Fortress Press, 1995).

[6] Hamrick, "Ezra-Nehemiah," 470–71.

[7] H. G. M. Williamson, *Ezra, Nehemiah*, in Word Biblical Commentary, vol. 16 (Waco: Word Books, 1985) 260.

[8] Hamrick, "Ezra-Nehemiah," 489.

Chapter 8

Joel

J. Hardy Kennedy wrote, "The book of Joel is the record of one such calamity and the consequent human suffering... The book has a timeless quality of point and pertinence for every generation and for every new experience of deep distress."[1] The final section of this commentary will focus on books that are believed to be written during or after the postexilic period, but the exact dating of these works is uncertain and still debated. These works are described aptly as "timeless" truths because they speak with efficacy regardless of their exact location in a historical context. These five remaining works include Joel, Jonah, Song of Songs, Esther, and Daniel.

During the time of the postexilic period, the earlier texts of prophecy were read and interpreted anew for their contemporary generation. This phenomenon led to the development of works such as Joel. The words of Joel are not intuitive, but rather are the collection and response to earlier prophetic utterings. A quick reading of Joel alerts the reader to the author's use and reinterpretation of several existing prophetic texts: Joel 2:2 is from Zephaniah 1:15; Joel 2:6 is from Nahum 2:10; Joel 2:32 corresponds to Obadiah 17; Joel 3:18 is taken from Amos 9:13; and Joel 2:11, 31 come from Malachi 3:2 and 4:5. A previous generation of scholars commonly dated Joel, along with Hosea and Amos, in the seventh or eighth century BCE due to its insertion between these works in the Hebrew canon. Current scholarship seems more comfortable with a relatively late date for Joel. Joel 3:2 describes a time when Judah has been sold into slavery and is scattered, a probable reference to the exile. References to the temple in 1:14 and 2:17 are probably referring to the rebuilt second temple, which was rededicated in 515 BCE, and the walls of Jerusalem have been rebuilt according to 2:9, following the work of Ezra and Nehemiah in 444 BCE. Thus, an estimated date for Joel is probably somewhere between 400–350 BCE.

The Hebrew version differs from the English versions of Joel in chapter and versification. There are four chapters of Joel in the Hebrew version compared to the three in our English texts. The Hebrew version divides the verses between 1:1-20, 2:1-27, 3:1-5, and 4:1-21. This is just the opposite of what we find in the book of Malachi, which reduces the number of chapters from four in our English versions to three in the Hebrew version.

Joel serves as an Old Testament writing that bridges the gap between the world of prophetic and apocalyptic literature. While Joel is firmly entrenched among the prophetic literature of Israel, it also contains apocalyptic features in the same tradition as Ezekiel 38–39, Daniel 7–12, and Zechariah 9–14. The main vision of this brief work, the vision of the locusts, is used as a symbol referring to the coming Day of the Lord. Several verses describe apocalyptic events. Joel 2:1 says the Day of the Lord is near. A time of judgment is mentioned in 3:12. God's coming appearance is described in terms of a theophany in 2:10, 2:30-31, and 3:15. Joel 3:9-12 mentions a coming war, culminating in an age of peace and absence of war as described in 2:27 and 3:18.

Little is known about the prophet named Joel. The superscription in Joel 1:1 says that Joel is the recipient of the word of the Lord and his father is named Pethuel. The Syriac and Greek versions of this verse change the spelling of the name Pethuel from a "P" to a "B." A Bethuel, who was the father of Rebekah, is found in Genesis 22:22-23. The name Joel means "Yahweh is God" in Hebrew. There are twelve other persons who are identified with the name Joel in other Old Testament passages. The repeated references in Joel to the temple suggest that Joel is a prophet who lived in or near Jerusalem (1:14, 16; 2:17). Joel also makes frequent reference to the priesthood and the offerings (1:9, 13; 2:14). Thus, we can infer that Joel lived in or near Jerusalem and is concerned with the religious life of Israel and her priests.

The Day of the Lord

The Day of the Lord is a repeated theme throughout the prophetic literature of the Old Testament. Amos 5:18-20 records,

> Alas for you who desire the day of the Lord!
>   Why do you want the day of the Lord?
> It is darkness, not light;
>   as if someone fled from a lion,
>   and was met by a bear;
> or went into the house and rested a hand against the wall,
>   and was bitten by a snake.
> Is not the day of the Lord darkness, not light,
>   and gloom with no brightness in it?

Students of Dr. Jerry Wallace, a long-time religion faculty member and former president of Campbell University, a Baptist university in the tiny hamlet of Buies Creek, North Carolina, will recognize the Hebrew phrase *Yom Yahweh*. Dr. Wallace would always refer to his upcoming tests as the *Yom Yahweh*, or "Day of the Lord." Dr. Wallace's usage of this term is very much in line with the Old Testament understanding of this phrase. It is a day of judgment. For those who are ready, the judgment will be a time of affirmation and praise. For those who are not ready, it will be day for gnashing of teeth and great anxiety.

The coming of the Day of the Lord represents the primary theme of the book of Joel. This phrase only appears in the Old Testament sixteen times. Five of the references to the Day of the Lord are found in the book of Joel. At the heart of this image is the God of Israel bringing judgment upon the enemies of Israel, standing as a divine warrior and judge who crushes all who would oppose. In the aforementioned passage of Amos 5:18-20, Amos chides the people of the northern kingdom, Israel, who affirm that the coming of the Day of the Lord will be a glorious day for the people of Israel. Amos reminds them that God's justice casts a powerful light on all who turn from the ways of God. The people are admonished for their misunderstanding of what the Day of the Lord is meant to be.

In one way, Joel is clarifying more precisely what the Day of the Lord will be. It will be both a day of judgment and deliverance for Israel. Joel describes the Day of the Lord in terms of the natural disaster of locusts coming upon the people as a device aiding in the people's return to God in a cry for help. There are at least two obvious lessons for today's readers. One parallel is to simply mention the prevalence of literature calling or even longing for the Lord's return today. We assume that it, too, will be a great day of rejoicing and victory for those in the Christian faith. Is this idea really that different than what is described by Amos or Joel? Woe to those of us who think we have God and all of God's plans figured out because of our charts, diagrams, and singular reading of a few choice texts. I am afraid that Amos's warning above has great application in our world today. Another parallel is also inherent in the warning to be prepared for the Day of the Lord. May we live with a heart for anticipation, but with arms of action and labor while there is still time to make a difference in the world in which we live. The Day of the Lord did come in one sense in the person of Jesus Christ, the Messiah. In Christ there is both judgment and deliverance. Be wary of those who continue to long for the coming Day of the Lord—it just might be a difficult exam like those in Dr. Wallace's classroom!

The Texts of Joel

Joel 1:1–2:27

Joel 1:1–2:27 describes a massive invasion of locusts into the land of Judah. Joel is described as a messenger in Joel 1:1. He is not delivering his own thoughts on the tragedy before him, but rather serving as God's messenger or intermediary between the God of Israel and the people. Joel calls upon the people to mark the severity of the plague in 1:2-3. It is a generational event that will not soon be forgotten. Several years ago, residents of the Southeast were inundated by cicadas, locust-like creatures that emerge to prey on vegetation every seventeen years. They were everywhere. Though not truly related to the locust, the cicada takes its name from the Latin for "tree cricket." We have twenty-seven pear trees that line our driveway up our rather steep hill. I returned from being away to discover these blessed cicada creatures were literally six to ten deep on top of each other covering our pear trees. They were loud and a nuisance. Fortunately, they did not do the damage that some locusts are capable of, but it did remind me of the many times that plagues of locusts are mentioned in the Old Testament and what those poor folks had to deal with. Plagues of locusts pose a much greater danger as they can destroy entire plantings of the fields and crops, bringing famine upon the people. Joel 1:4 describes such a scenario. The vegetation necessary for food is gone, eaten by these swarming creatures.

The prophet Joel calls for a time of national mourning and lament because of the devastation brought upon by the locusts. Joel calls for a time of fasting and repentance, linking this plague as a sign of God's disfavor with the people. In v. 15 the plague is connected to the nearness of the coming Day of the Lord. Joel calls upon God in vv. 19-and 20 to deliver them from this time of famine and drought.

Joel is following the example set in the book of Hosea. Hosea establishes the scenario of an unfaithful wife in Hosea 1–3 and uses this unfaithfulness as an allegory for the message of the book that follows in Hosea 4–14, contending that Israel has been unfaithful to God. Joel begins with the description of the terrible plague of locusts, then quickly moves in Joel 2:1-2 to interpreting the plague as a sign of the nearness of the coming Day of the Lord. Joel compares the invasion of locusts to the image of an invading army with God leading them, as described in v. 11. This day is described in terms of a theophany, or appearance of God. In v. 10 the earth shakes, the sky trembles, the sun and moon grow dark, and the stars withhold their brilliance. God is pictured thundering before this coming army.

Joel 2:12-17 is a call for repentance in an attempt to avert disaster. The locusts are leveraged as more than just a naturally occurring event, but instead are seen as a sign of God's judgment upon the land. Joel calls upon the people to lead in a national time of repentance. Rending their hearts and not their clothes is mentioned in v. 13. Verse 13 also draws attention to the mercy of God as "slow to anger, and abounding in steadfast love." Joel calls upon all people to a measure of true humility and contriteness, not just an outward show or display of religious fervor. He calls upon the young, the elderly, those being given in marriage, and the priests to humble themselves before God in actions of true repentance.

God responds positively to the national repentance of the people (v. 18). As a result, God promises to drive the locusts' swarm, again described as an army, out into the desert and into the eastern (Dead Sea) and western (Mediterranean) seas. Verses 21-27 describe the restoration that is already begun with the renewal of pastureland, trees full of fruit, and vines once again yielding their crops. The people are promised to have plenty once again. This section ends with a promise that seems vacuous in some ways as one considers the history of the Jewish people: "And my people shall never again be put to shame" (v. 27b). Margaret Dee Bratcher describes this verse as a fitting conclusion to this oracle: "Verse 27, the climax in this proclamation of salvation, speaks to the larger theological issue of Israel's relationship to Yahweh: Israel will acknowledge and experience the presence of Yahweh in its midst and his exaltation as the one true God."[2] The people will once again survive. A day is coming when the people will know the joys and security of living in an ongoing relationship with their God.

JOEL

Joel 2:28–3:21

Joel now shifts his focus from the plague of locusts to engaging the theme of the coming Day of the Lord, describing what that day will be like. In some ways Joel 2:28–3:21 is simply an expansion of the prophecy of salvation mentioned in Joel 2:18-27. The coming Day of the Lord will be a day of blessing for the righteous ones. God's spirit will be poured out on all people, and all people will have a relationship with God. Sons and daughters will proclaim God's word. Young and old will enjoy this fellowship, and there will be no exclusion of individuals based on gender. Joel 2:28-32 is quoted by the author of Acts to describe the events of the coming of the Holy Spirit at Pentecost (2:17-21). The author of Acts seems to be indicating that the Day of the Lord had arrived with the coming of Jesus, his ascension, and the formal giving of the Holy Spirit upon the people. As Joel describes the coming Day of the Lord as a day of experiencing relationship with God, the author of Acts demonstrates the ability of this relationship with the indwelling of God's spirit in the life of the believer.

Further blessings on Israel and the righteous ones include the restoration of the prominence of Jerusalem and God's vow of protection for the city once again in 3:16-17. Jerusalem is described as a stronghold for the people. God states that Jerusalem will once again be holy, or separate, inviolable to outside threat of invasion. The issue of the inviolability of Jerusalem was a constant thread in the writings of Isaiah of Jerusalem. The picture of a renewal of Jerusalem is also reminiscent of the rich imagery contained in Ezekiel 40–48, which describes the new temple and how Jerusalem would arise following the exile. New wine and a land flowing with milk and water are further described in v. 18. Joel describes the coming Day of the Lord as a day of great blessing for those who live in a right relationship before God.

The coming Day of the Lord will not be a pleasant day for the wicked, though. Joel 3:1-3 states that the nations will be judged based on how they have treated Israel. This judgment will take place at the "Valley of Jehoshaphat," or "Valley of the

Lord's judgment." The Day of the Lord is a day of reckoning. Those who have lived as enemies to God's people will be held accountable for their misdeeds. Joel 3:9-15 describes a terrible war between the warriors of God and the nations who have persecuted Israel. Joel does not provide any details about this battle or war except to describe the call to battle and then follows with a description of the outcome. In Joel 3:19-21 the enemies of God and Israel will be laid waste. Egypt and Edom are mentioned by name in v. 19. Egypt was an ongoing nemesis for the Israelites, dating back to the events of the exodus with the preceding years of captivity. Egypt also continues to reoccur in the pages of Israel's sacred text in many scenes, most recently as the land engaged in war with Babylon, which led to the eventual destruction of Judah and the taking of the elite inhabitants of Judah into captivity. The Edomites were the descendants of Esau and were blood kin to the nation of Israel. Throughout their history a blood feud was maintained between Israel and Edom. Texts dealing with the destruction of Jerusalem at the hands of the Babylonians mention the Edomites taking advantage of the weakened condition of Judah to pillage and plunder her brother nation and people.

Joel 3:20-21 ends with a beautiful promise of hope. Jerusalem and the inhabitants of Judah will be pardoned. The text ends with a powerful statement of God's presence: "The LORD dwells in Zion."

Conclusion

Joel may only be three chapters in the English version, but these three chapters are filled with words of hope and encouragement that are indeed a timeless truth. Joel uses a natural disaster as his introduction to call the people of Judah back to faith in God and instills anticipation once again for the coming of the Day of the Lord. Joel 2:28–3:21 provides one of the fullest commentaries on what the Day of the Lord actually is—a day of hope and calamity. Though brief, Joel offers hope and comfort for a people who are suffering and points them to a brighter day, a day of restoration and ongoing relationship with the God of Israel.

For Further Reading

Ballard, Harold W. *The Divine Warrior Motif in the Psalms* (Richland Hills TX: The Berkeley Institute of Biblical and Archaeological Literature, 1999).

Bratcher, Margaret Dee. "Joel." *The Prophets: Mercer Commentary on the Bible*, vol. 4. Macon GA: Mercer University Press, 1996.

Blenkinsopp, Joseph. *A History of Prophecy in Israel*. Louisville: Westminster John Knox Press, 1996.

Kennedy, J. Hardy. "Joel." *The Broadman Bible Commentary*, vol. 7. Nashville: Broadman Press, 1972.

Von Rad, Gerhard. *The Message of the Prophets*. San Francisco: HarperSanFrancisco, 1965.

West, James King. *Introduction to the Old Testament*. New York: Macmillan Publishing Company, 1981.

Notes

[1] J. Hardy Kennedy, "Joel," in *The Broadman Bible Commentary*, vol. 7 (Nashville: Broadman Press, 1972) 61.

[2] Margaret Dee Bratcher, "Joel," in *The Prophets: Mercer Commentary on the Bible*, vol. 4 (Macon GA: Mercer University Press, 1996) 266.

Chapter 9

Jonah

Jonah is one of those books we simply set aside because we heard the story of Jonah when we were children and the story hasn't changed. In fact, if we were to package the story of Jonah on its own merits, apart from the pages of the Old Testament, and distribute it to our local bookstores, we would probably find the book relegated to the children's section of books. The fantastic story of a fish swallowing a man reminds us of *Pinocchio*, or the fast-growing plant reminds us of the story of *Jack and the Beanstalk*. This great book, however, offers timeless truths for readers of all ages. It is also part of the collection of writings that we as persons of faith deem as God's word to humanity, exalting it as sacred literature.

Jonah was a historical figure from the eighth century BCE, according to 2 Kings 14:23-27, which mentions Jonah, the son of Amittai, who served as a prophet during the days of Jeroboam II in the northern kingdom of Israel. Jonah was from Gaph-Hepher, a small village about three miles northeast of Nazareth. This verse associates Jonah with the expansion of the northern kingdom's borders to its greatest extent since the days of King Solomon. Thus, the longstanding traditional approach views the book as a record of the events of this eighth-century prophet.

Most modern scholarship views Jonah as a short story or novella with nationalistic overtones, created around the end of the fifth or beginning of the fourth century BCE, basing the story on a little-known prophet named Jonah. This allows the author of the story to fashion a carefully aimed message to the people of Israel. The word *Yonah* means "dove" in biblical Hebrew and has been used on many occasions as the national symbol for the nation of Israel. Whether you interpret the book of Jonah as a purely historical record of an eighth-century prophet or as a literary creation in the fifth or fourth century, the message remains essentially intact—God loves all people and desires all people to know God's salvation. Jonah's message is relegated to five words in Hebrew, translated in Jonah 3:4b, "Forty days more, and Nineveh shall be overthrown!" Remarkably, the people of Nineveh respond in repentance to Jonah's call for spiritual change.

The book of Jonah is divided into two parts. Part one tells of Jonah's adventure in running away from the call of God on a ship in the opposite direction of Nineveh in Jonah 1 and 2. Part two continues with the story, following Jonah as he goes to Nineveh, delivers the message he has received, then camps on a hill overlooking the city as he waits for God's wrath to come upon the inhabitants of the city. Both parts of Jonah follow the same literary paradigm. First, Jonah is commissioned to deliver a message to Nineveh (1:2; 3:2). Second, both parts picture Gentiles who are more receptive to God's message than the prophet of Israel (1:14-16; 3:6-10). Third, both parts conclude with Jonah alone with God (2:2-10; 4:9-11).

The form of the writing of Jonah is primarily in Hebrew prose or narrative. In other words, it is a story. The prayer of Jonah recorded in Jonah 2:2-9, however, is a psalm of thanksgiving and is written in poetic form. As a literary exercise I encourage you to reread Jonah, deleting the poem in Jonah 2:2-9 in order to experience firsthand the story of Jonah in a purely narrative form. The prayer does add to the story of Jonah, as it demonstrates a change of heart in the prophet, directing praise to the God of Israel for deliverance. It also extols God for a second chance in performing the task that God has laid before him.

JONAH

The Texts of Jonah
Jonah 1:1-17

Fans of the popular 1970s BBC television series *Monty Python's Flying Circus* will remember the use of the term "run away" in the theater troop's movie *Monty Python and the Holy Grail*. Throughout the film, the company of pilgrims, led by legendary King Arthur on a quest to recover the Holy Grail, find themselves in peril, and their ultimate battle cry becomes "Run away!" In Jonah 1 we find this eighth-century northern prophet choosing to "run away" rather than complete the task that God has placed before him.

In Jonah 1:1-3 God initiates the plan brought to Jonah. God has called Jonah to be God's emissary to the people of Nineveh, a large city that once served as the capital of Assyria, the hated enemies of Israel. Jonah is called to deliver a call to repentance to the people of Nineveh on behalf of the God of Israel. Jonah balks at this request. The Assyrians were a ruthless, warlike Middle Eastern power who ultimately destroy Israel, laying waste to Samaria in 722 BCE.

The reader learns that Jonah is the son of Amittai, which is the Hebrew word for "my truth." We know nothing else about the personal life of Jonah apart from Jonah 1:1 and possibly 2 Kings 14:25. Jonah's call is explicit: "Go at once to Nineveh . . . and cry out against it" (v. 2). Nineveh was an important city in ancient Assyria. It became the capital of Assyria in the late eighth century when the seat of power was moved from the city of Asshur to Nineveh long after the days of Jeroboam II, the Israelite king also mentioned in 2 Kings 14:25. There was no doubt or guesswork in Jonah's call. God called Jonah to a very specific task: Go and tell!

Jonah responds to God's call to go to Nineveh by running in the other direction. Verse 3 says that Jonah "set out to flee to Tarshish." There has been much speculation about where Tarshish was in Jonah's day. The traditional understanding is that Tarshish was located in southern Spain. W. F. Albright suggests the name Tarshish meant "refinery or smelter," as in a place where metal was smelted. Norman Snaith suggests Tarshish meant "to the farthest west, or the end of the world." Cyrus Gordon suggested it means "a far-off, and sometimes idealized port that cannot be identified with any one location. . . . In literature and popular legends it became a distant paradise."[1] God called Jonah to go east to preach to the people of Nineveh, but Jonah chose to go west, toward a distant port, away from the call set before him.

Jonah 1:4-16 details the experience of Jonah's flight away from God and from the responsibilities placed before him. Jonah, who is recognized as a nationalistic prophet, finds himself among a ship's crew of sailors who are presumably not Jewish, or worshipers of the God of Israel. Verse 4 credits God with sending a great wind against the ship. The Hebrew word for wind is *ruach*, the same word used for "breath" or "spirit." In one sense God blows up the wind against the plans and direction of the rebellious prophet Jonah. There is rich irony in the picture of the pagan captain calling upon Jonah the Israelite to call upon his god. A. J. Glazer writes, "The recipient of the universal truth remained in the stupor of sleep while the heathen worked feverishly and hopelessly for their salvation."[2]

The ancient mariners cast lots to determine who on board might be responsible for the wrath of the gods falling upon them on the open seas. The practice of casting lots is an ancient practice of divination, or trying to determine the will of a divine through a physical object. The practice of divination was common in the ancient Middle East and was also a common practice among the prophets of Israel. Hepatoscopy, or seeing the liver of a deceased animal, was another common practice of divination in ancient times. The sailors cast lots and determine that Jonah is the offending party. The sailors inquire of Jonah if there is something he has done to bring about the calamity upon them. In v. 9 Jonah confesses his faith in God even as he is also guilty of running away from God's call. He instructs the sailors to toss him overboard to appease God and to ease God's anger against them. Verse 13 records that even when they recognized the offending party, the men

JONAH

tried to row again toward land. The "pagan" sailors did not abandon Jonah without first trying to save his life. Finally, after their efforts of return are fruitless, the sailors deliver Jonah to the sea. In v. 16 the sailors vow to the God of Israel and offer sacrifices to God. Even in Jonah's disobedience, God is portrayed at work. God often takes the most ugly, dire circumstances of our lives and turns them into something beautifully redemptive.

The story of Jonah is most famous for the event described in Jonah 1:17: "But the LORD provided a large fish to swallow up Jonah; and Jonah was in the belly of the fish three days and three nights." Some like to rant and rave about how God accomplished the miraculous feat of a fish swallowing a person whole, all the while preserving Jonah's life. The story of Jonah, however, is much greater than the task of a fish swallowing a man. The Hebrew text uses the word, *dag*, or "fish." The Greek translation calls this creature a large fish, or whale. Others see Jonah's misadventure as a messianic prediction of Jesus Christ being in the pits of Sheol for three days and then being resurrected, but the imperfect Jonah is far removed as an archetype for Jesus Christ. To spend so much energy over the question of "Did he, or didn't he?" is to miss the true meaning of the message of Jonah. The message of Jonah is about God's love for ALL people, and God's call to us to be open to ALL people, especially those we perceive as unworthy or even our sworn enemies. The message is not "Could God really have created a fish or whale that large?" or "If God did, could a person really survive the event?"

Several years ago my family and I had the pleasure of going on a whale-watching expedition off the coast of New Hampshire and Maine. It was a wonderful experience being on a small boat approximately twenty-five miles out in the Atlantic Ocean. Throughout the morning we saw no signs of the large mammals we were pursuing. Finally, when the boats' crew was about to give up and return to shore, we ran across several fifty- to sixty-foot whales playfully swimming alongside the boat. I have no doubt, since I affirm God as the divine creator, that God would have little trouble creating a fish, hamster, penguin, or whatever God chose large enough to swallow a person whole. My appreciation for Jonah, however, rests not in that question, but rather in "What does God want me to understand from this story?" Jonah would not accept a very important truth—ALL people matter to God. The purpose of the fish in the story is not designed as a litmus test for the faith of the believer. The fish is merely a vessel used by God to help Jonah get back on the right path once again. What does it take for God to help us find our way back to the path of following God's call in our lives?

Jonah 2:1-10

Fishing is a great sport enjoyed by millions of people worldwide. My father and sister were the big "fisher people" of my family. My sister and I would sometimes accompany my dad to work when he worked at the Port of Muskogee on the banks of the Arkansas River in Oklahoma. We would take our fishing poles and sit on the gangplanks or sometimes off the barges and fish for hours on end. One day my sister caught the biggest crappie I have ever seen. It took her several minutes to wrestle the fish over to me on the bank. She was fishing off the gangplank and swung her line over to me on the shore. As I was taking this large crappie off of her hook, the fish began to squirm, and I dropped her potential trophy fish back into the river! She burst into tears and began to scream, "You dropped our lunch!"

At the end of Jonah 1, Jonah is swallowed by a great fish. In Jonah 2 the reader is privy to a prayer attributed implicitly to Jonah after the event itself has taken place. This prayer is a psalm of thanksgiving, emphasizing Jonah's repentance and turning back to the God of Israel. Verses 1 and 10 serve as a parenthesis to this psalm written in narrative form. The message of the psalm could easily be shortened to the theme "God can get us out of any mess!" Some scholars see the relationship between this psalm of thanksgiving and the narrative framework as being out of order; some believe the passage reads better when you read vv. 1 and 10 first, then follow it with

vv. 2-9. There are two main sections to Jonah 2. Verses 1-6 detail the mess Jonah finds himself in. Verses 7-10 celebrate God's deliverance from this slimy situation. There is a slight adjustment in the versification between our English translations and the Hebrew Bible. Verse 1:17 actually is the first verse of chapter 2 in the Hebrew version of Jonah.

In Jonah 2:1, Jonah finds himself inside the fish, but as the story goes, he is amazed to learn that he is still alive. The story emphasizes the unpleasantness that often awaits persons of faith who turn from following God's path in their lives. Are all of our problems caused by God? By no means is this true, but there are many stories throughout the Bible describing God using the obstacles found in life as beacons guiding God's children back onto the right path. In this predicament Jonah finally acknowledges and cries out to God. In v. 4 Jonah cries that he has been banished from the very sight of God. We sometimes remove ourselves from the course that God has laid before us by our sinful actions and rebellion against God. The truth is that we can never separate ourselves from God's care, presence, and desire to care for us in the midst of despondency (Rom 8:38-39). In the midst of the sea, in the belly of a fish, in the dark of the night, God is there! Jonah finally recognizes his need for God in the midst of this awful situation: "I called to the LORD out of my distress, and he answered me" (v. 2a).

The second half of this psalm of thanksgiving emphasizes God's deliverance. Verse 7 states, "As my life was ebbing away, I remembered the LORD; and my prayer came to you, into your holy temple." The Hebrew word for "remember," *zakar*, is a prominent word in the Hebrew Bible. It is the theme of Deuteronomy as Moses calls the Israelites to remember their God as they travel into the promised land. In his time of consternation, Jonah thinks about the one who is able to deliver him—God—and vows to make good on his pledge to complete the task before him. Vows were to be taken seriously in the narratives of the Old Testament.

Reverend M. E. Fitzpatrick, known to his friend as "Fitz," was the first pastor I worked with in a full-time ministry situation. Fitz often spoke of his life experience as part of an

American bomber crew during World War II. Fitz was assigned duty on a Flying Fortress and served a full tour of duty in the European theater. During his tour of duty, Fitz vowed before God that if God would allow him to return home, he would serve him the rest of his days in the work of ministry. I had a front-row seat as Fitz retired from faithful service of thirty-five years as a pastor of a local church. He was faithful to his vow before God.

"Deliverance belongs to the LORD," Jonah 2:9 affirms. God can indeed deliver us from any mess we may find ourselves in. Most of us will never find ourselves dodging shrapnel or being trapped inside the belly of a great fish, but our messes matter to God. You matter to God. This psalm of thanksgiving reminds us that God can rescue us from any mess, even if we, like Jonah, find ourselves in messes of our own creation: "Then the LORD spoke to the fish, and it spewed Jonah out upon the dry land" (v. 10).

Jonah 3:1-10

In Jonah 3, Jonah finally gets to the destination he has been charged to address. Jonah also gets a second chance from God. Not to be overly cliché, but God is pictured in the story of Jonah as a God of second chances. The second chance is extended not just for the prophet Jonah, but also for the entire city of Nineveh. Verse 3 describes Nineveh as a very large city, taking three days to go through it. Archaeology suggests the ancient city of Nineveh was less than eight miles in total circumference. It is described as three miles long and one and a half miles wide. The word "large" can be translated as "great," thus speaking of the city's importance and not of its physical size.

Jonah's message is direct in v. 4b: "Forty days more, and Nineveh shall be overthrown!" Not a fancy message, but straight to the point. Verses 5-10 record the response of the people. Verse 5 states that the people believed this message to be a word of God to them. They respond by declaring a fast and putting on the traditional garments of mourning or repentance, sackcloth. The king responds in v. 6 by personally participating in this time of repentance and issuing a decree, calling upon the people to fast and pray for forgiveness. Even the animals were to be included in this time of city-wide fasting (v. 8). In v. 10 we learn that "God saw what they did." God chooses to respond with compassion, sparing the lives of the king, the people of the city, and the livestock. The Hebrew word for compassion used in Jonah 4:10 is the same word repeated twice at the beginning of the call of Deutero-Isaiah in Isaiah 40:1, *nacham*, which means to "be sorry, repent, or have compassion for."

The reluctant prophet has faithfully delivered his message, the people have responded, and God has heard their cries, sparing the city of Nineveh from destruction. This would seem like a fitting conclusion to the story of Jonah, but it does not end here.

Jonah 4:1-11

We see Jonah waiting for the main event of hellfire and brimstone to destroy the city of Nineveh in Jonah 4. The late senator Sam J. Ervin from Morganton, North Carolina, once said, "I once knew a preacher back home who liked to use words that he sometimes didn't quite understand. One time he brought in a visiting preacher, and after introducing him to the congregation, he told him to preach very loud, because the agnostics in this church are not very good."[3] One should be very careful about how language is used and what is actually communicated by one's speech and action.

I once had a pastor who also sometimes used words for which he didn't quite know the meaning. One Sunday, when commenting on the success of our church softball team, this preacher referred to the men of the team as a great bunch of "morphodites," a word his elementary children had been using at school. Most of you will recognize the word "hermaphrodite" as a person who has the physical features/characteristics of both male and female. Dr. Tom Wilks, a professor at Oklahoma Baptist University, was a member of our church.

The next Sunday following this declaration by our pastor, Tom gave the announcements from the pulpit. He began to tell the congregation that he had looked up the word "morphodite" and learned that it was a slang term for the word "hermaphrodite." The dictionary gave the definition as "a plant or animal having both male and female productive organs and secondary sexual characteristics." Tom also added that the dictionary had added that at the time of the writing of that particular dictionary, there were less than fifteen hermaphrodites known to be alive throughout the world. He added how fortunate we were to have twelve of the fifteen known cases worldwide to be going to our small country church. Again, I write, one must be very careful; the words we say and the things we do really can make an impact on our world.

Jonah had issued a warning to the people, and now Jonah was content to climb a local hill, sit back, and enjoy the destruction of his nation's enemies. Jonah had missed the purpose for his message. His actions do not describe a person acting with compassion, but rather a person carrying out strict instructions without a sense of personal caring for the possible victims of his message.

In Jonah 4:1-3, Jonah is upset because God has brought salvation to the hated enemies of Israel, the Assyrians. It was the Assyrians who destroyed Samaria, the capital of the northern kingdom, Israel, in 722 BCE. It was the Assyrians who had shut Ahaz and his prophet Isaiah inside the city of Jerusalem in 705 BCE. The Assyrians were ruthless people who were the natural enemies of all the smaller states that existed in the region of Palestine at this time. Jonah issues a word of self-pity: "O LORD, please take my life from me, for it is better for me to die than to live" (v. 3). Jonah's words seem extreme, but they demonstrate the great disdain he holds for the Assyrians. These words also give the reader a glimpse into the immaturity of Jonah, who did not care at all for the people of this large city.

God responds to Jonah with two questions in vv. 4 and 9. God asks Jonah if he has any right to be angry with the grace God has afforded the people of Nineveh. What is it to us who

God chooses to bless, to curse, to pardon, or to destroy? I have recently seen two interesting bumper stickers. One reads, "Jesus is coming soon, and boy is he mad!" The second reads, "A vote for _____ is a vote for Satan." It seems to me that both of these unrelated bumper stickers personify what I would call the "Jonah effect." It is too easy to place ourselves in the seat of judgment.

The theme of jealousy over God's vindication and judgment is a recurring theme in the parables told by Jesus. In the story of the prodigal son in Luke 15, the older brother is angry that his father has welcomed home the prodigal, bestowing such lavish rewards on him, while he the faithful older brother has received nothing. Matthew 20:1-16 relates the parable of the workers who were paid the same amount as those who came to work at later times throughout the day. Those who came earlier complained about not being treated fairly, but Jesus reiterated that all were the same in God's kingdom. In fact, the first would be seen as the last, and the last would be considered as the first. These parables remind us that the love of God is for ALL humanity, not just a chosen few.

Jonah 4:5-8 records Jonah's response to God's act of mercy. Jonah builds a shelter east of the city to sit back and watch the main event. God produces a vine to provide additional shading for Jonah. But after the vine grows, God sends a worm that causes the vine to wither. God then sends a scorching east wind and heat from the sun, making Jonah miserable. Jonah reiterates the call for his own life to end, saying, "It is better for me to die than to live" (v. 8b). Once again, like the entire story of Jonah, the author provides a parable-like story to carry across his or her message to the reader. Jonah is more worried about his personal comfort and the loss of a temporary vine than he is about the welfare of an entire city of people. The message is reiterated with one final push! God loves EVERYONE and wishes for none to perish! Jonah hated that God offered grace to the people of Nineveh. God has the final word to Jonah in the story: "Should I not be concerned about Nineveh?" (v. 11).

Conclusion

Jonah's message of inclusivism represents one of the last prophetic voices in the Old Testament. The message is quite clear: The covenant God made with Abraham in Genesis was to be a vehicle by which God could bring salvation to all the nations. God is just as concerned with the enemies of Israel as God is with Israel herself. As previously mentioned in our discussion of the book of Joel, it appears that many today are sitting on that eastern hillside waiting for the main event. For Joel the main event was the coming of the Day of the Lord; for Jonah it was the destruction that God promised to bring upon the people of Nineveh. What are you waiting for God to do in our world today?

The story of Jonah demonstrates the problems with the narrow view of God and God's love that had become prominent in Israel's theology. Jonah represents the attitude of the nation of Israel. How could God possibly care about a nation of Gentiles, the sworn enemies of Israel? Jonah is also portrayed as a hypocrite. He himself experiences the forgiveness and restoration offered by God but becomes angry when that same forgiveness is offered to others. There is much to learn from the book of Jonah, but mostly these lessons come in the form of bad examples. There could be a subtitle or disclaimer that reads, "The views of management may not be reflected by the words and actions of the title character of this story." The story does teach the reader about the nature of God. God is portrayed as merciful and forgiving and as one who chooses love rather than judgment. God's love is available to all. Jonah challenges the narrow nationalism so prevalent in postexilic theology. Jonah challenges Israel to be a light to the nations.

For Further Reading

Blenkinsopp, Joseph. *A History of Prophecy in Israel.* Louisville: Westminster John Knox Press, 1996.

Craig, Kenneth M. "Jonah." *The Prophets: Mercer Commentary on the Bible*, vol. 4. Macon GA: Mercer University Press, 1996.

Glaze, A. J. "Jonah." *The Broadman Bible Commentary*, vol. 7. Nashville: Broadman Press, 1972.

Limburg, James. *Jonah*. The Old Testament Library. Louisville: Westminster John Knox Press, 1993.

Matthews, Victor H. and James C. Moyer. *The Old Testament: Text and Context*. Peabody MA: Hendrickson Publishers, 1997.

Miller, John W. *Meet the Prophets: A Beginner's Guide to the Books of the Biblical Prophets*. New York: Paulist Press, 1987.

Soggin, J. Alberto. *Introduction to the Old Testament*. The Old Testament Library. Philadelphia: Westminster Press, 1989.

Von Rad, Gerhard. *The Message of the Prophets*. San Francisco: HarperSanFrancisco, 1965.

Notes

[1] A. J. Glaze, "Jonah," in *The Broadman Bible Commentary*, vol. 7 (Nashville: Broadman Press, 1972) 161.

[2] Ibid., 162.

[3] Loyal Jones and Billy Edd Wheeler, *Hometown Humor* (Little Rock: August House Publishers, 1991) 112.

Chapter 10

Song of Songs

The five writings known as the *Megilloth*, "scrolls," or more precisely "festal scrolls," have been grouped together since Talmudic times when the custom arose to read each of them publicly at one of the annual religious festivals. The five writings as they appear in the Hebrew Bible are Ruth, Songs of Songs, Ecclesiastes, Lamentations, and Esther. Ruth is generally read at the festival of Pentecost, which occurs annually during May or June. Song of Songs is read at the Passover during March or April. Ecclesiastes is associated with the Feast of Tabernacles, or Booths, during September or October. Lamentations is appropriately used during the commemoration of the ninth of Ab during July or August. The ninth of Ab is the saddest day in the Jewish calendar, as it calls the Jewish people to remember the destruction of the first and second temples along with many other subsequent horrors the people of Israel have suffered over the centuries. More recently, the ninth of Ab serves as the principal time of remembrance for the *Shoah*, or Holocaust. As one would naturally suspect, Esther is read during the festival of Purim, which takes place annually in February or March. Apart from their respective roles in liturgical use, these books share very little in common. They are spread out throughout different places in the texts of the Old Testament; thus, their place as part of the *Megilloth* is lost in our English Old Testament.[1]

The Song of Songs, also known as the Song of Solomon or Canticles, is one of the most problematic books in the entire Old Testament. Song of Songs 1:1 ascribes the book to Solomon. Solomon is also mentioned in various parts of the book, including 3:9, 3:11, and 8:11-12. Solomon is affirmed as the author of this work through a longstanding tradition. Most scholars today do not affirm Solomon as the author for several reasons. For one, there are many Aramaic phrases found throughout the book. This by itself would not be convincing evidence, but these phrases are also paired with a few Persian and Greek loan words that crop up in the text. Since Solomon reigned in the area of 960–920 BCE, the likelihood that Solomon would have any access to the language of Persia, which arose in the sixth century BCE, or ancient Greece, which came to power in the mid-fourth century BCE, seems highly unlikely. The text itself also does not read as a solitary story or poem. It appears to be a collection of many different poems from differing sources. Scholars today frequently assign a possible date as late as the Hellenistic era or third century BCE to Song of Songs.

Another area that proves particularly problematic for this book is the issue of interpretation. How are we to read this book, and how are we to make application of these words in our world today? From the beginning Song of Songs appears to have proved problematic for the early rabbinic councils and groups who formally and informally helped mold the canon of the Old Testament. It appears the early rabbis began to interpret this work allegorically as a picture of God's love for Israel. Early Christians had little problem adapting this allegorical approach to the Song of Songs, simply supplanting the church for the nation of Israel. Indeed, many modern editions of Bibles in English have parenthetical notes describing Christ's love for the church throughout the texts of Song of Songs. In my Thompson Chain Reference Bible, an editorial description over the text of Song of Songs 7 reads, "A further description of the graces of the church."[2] As one reads Song of Songs 7:6-8, one encounters the following words: "How fair and pleasant you are, O loved one, delectable maiden! You are stately as a palm tree, and your breasts are like its clusters. I say I will climb the palm tree and lay hold of its branches. O may your breasts be like clusters of the vine, and the scent of your breath like apples." Needless-to-say, when one reads Song of Songs 7, it is difficult to focus upon Christ's love for the church! Without the option of reading Song of Songs allegorically, this text may not have been preserved as sacred Scripture.

James King West lists the other ways this text has been interpreted over the years. The allegorical approach represents the earliest approach used by the rabbis and the early church. Understanding the words of Song of Songs as a cultic myth is a second approach. A third approach is seeing the Song of Songs as a drama used in early worship. A fourth approach views the work as a solitary love poem between one man and one woman. There is a general consensus today in reading the Song of Songs as a collection of love poetry brought together from various sources.[3] As I read the text of Song of Songs, I am aware of the beauty that God has instilled in a proper relationship between a man and a woman who celebrate their own identities as sexual beings through the relationship of marriage. Our sexuality and the ability to love are tremendous gifts from God to humanity. Through sexuality we have the ability to propagate our race and fulfill the purpose for which God intended. God also blessed humanity with the ability to experience pleasure through this experience. It is another way that God created us to experience God's love through our expression of our love for each other.

I will never forget one of my first religion professors at Oklahoma Baptist University, the late Dr. Dick Rader. Dr. Rader had just returned from the mission field to take a job as a professor of religion at OBU during my freshman year in college. In one of our classes on Christian ethics, Dr. Rader gave a very simple lecture on sexuality that I will never forget. I regularly pass along to my university Old Testament classes a summation of Rader's lecture when covering the book of Song of Songs. Dr. Rader gave us a lesson on biblical sexuality with three points. First, sex is good. Second, sex is powerful. Finally, sex must be controlled. We are not animals, bound to our instincts like dogs or rabbits. We are responsible for our expressions of sexuality. God has provided a wonderful means for that expression in the confines of a loving and committed union called marriage. Song of Songs provides a glimpse into the expression of human sexuality during biblical times.

The Texts of Song of Songs

Song of Songs is written entirely in Hebrew poetry. As a collection of love poetry, it is a difficult book to outline. The poetry features dialogue between a primary male and female voice professing their mutual love. There are times when the reader hears the words given by an individual male or female speaker. At other times the words of a group of women called the daughters of Jerusalem are heard. When comparing outlines of various scholars, one quickly sees places of disagreement concerning where to divide the various components of this work. As a point of entry into the text, I am following the outline suggested by Tom Gledhill in his commentary *The Message of the Song of Songs*.[4]

1:1

The first verse of Song of Songs is a superscription. These "titles," common in Psalms and in prophetic literature, introduce a section of writing, a psalm, or in this case information about the content or authorship of the writing. The superscription is usually a later addition to the work. Scholars are generally agreed that the editor is ascribing authorship to Solomon in this case, but the work itself is written much later than the time of Solomon. Solomon is mentioned in a few places throughout the Song of Songs (such as 1:5; 3:7; 8:1). Solomon is also mentioned in 1 Kings 4:32 as a writer of poetry and songs. Ascribing the writing to Solomon affords the writing a credibility or authority that it may not have on its own merit. This appeal for authority based on ancient names is also witnessed in other late writings, particularly in the period between the closing of the Old Testament canon and the beginning of the New Testament canon.

The use of the Hebrew word *shir*, "a song," twice in the superscription serves as a superlative in the Hebrew language. It could be translated as "the best of all songs" or "the grandest song."

1:2–2:7

In this passage we encounter dialogue between a woman, often referred to with the editorial title "beloved," and a man, who is sometimes editorially described as the lover.[5] This first section details this exchange of mutual pleasantries, affirming their love for each other. In vv. 5-8 the woman attributes her dark hue to circumstances beyond her control. She speaks of her exposure to the effects of the wind and the sun due to her care for her vineyards. She has not lived a life of luxury, guarded from the harmful rays of the sun. She addresses her common station to the "daughters of Jerusalem," which may be a reference to a harem, choir, or chorus. Those who hold to Solomon as the author of this poem would no doubt see this phrase as a reference to Solomon's harem. We are not told specifically the identity of this chorus of women, but they do play an important role in the book. Tom Gledhill writes, "They [the daughters of Jerusalem] act as a foil, as a sounding board, for the expression of the girl's deepest feelings and emotions. They draw from the girl the articulation of her yearnings; seldom if at all do they play an active role in the drama."[6]

The phrase "lily of the valleys" harkens back to the text of Song of Songs 2:1, which reads, "I am a rose of Sharon, a lily of the valleys." The old English melody "The Lily of the Valley, may be very familiar to you. The words of the song are included here:

> I have found a friend in Jesus,
> > He's everything to me,
> > He's the fairest of ten thousand to my soul;
> The Lily of the Valley,

> In Him alone I see
> All I need to cleanse and make me fully whole.
> In sorrow He's my comfort,
> In trouble He's my stay,
> He tells me every care on Him to roll;
> He's the Lily of the Valley,
> The Bright and Morning Star,
> He's the Fairest of ten thousand to my soul.[7]

This is one of the many hymns I grew up singing in small rural Baptist congregations. Most of us have heard Jesus Christ referred to as the "lily of the valley" or the "rose of Sharon." What we haven't seen is where this title is used of Jesus in the New Testament. Simply put, it isn't there. This common designation of Jesus Christ comes as a direct result of the allegorical interpretation of the Song of Songs.

The word translated as "rose" in v. 1 is the Hebrew word *havatselet*, meaning "rose" or "flower." It only appears twice in the Hebrew Bible. Isaiah 35:1 records the second occurrence of this word. Some translations prefer to use the word "crocus." The rose of Sharon is a common name for either of two unrelated plants that are commonly found in Israel. One is also known as "Aaron's beard," or the gold flower, and the other is known as "Althaea." The species name is *Hibiscus Syriacus*. Somehow, saying Jesus is the *Hibiscus Syriacus* just doesn't roll off the tongue.

The word "lily," or *shoshanat* in Hebrew, appears four other places in the Old Testament: twice in 1 Kings, twice in the Song of Songs, and once in Hosea. The *convallaria majalis*, or "lily of the valley," is a perennial herb found in Eurasia and eastern North America and is popular in shady garden spots. Its tiny, bell-shaped white flowers are often used in the manufacturing of perfume. In our culture today, the Easter lily has attained the mark as the most recognizable of the varieties of lilies. Through the lens of a Christology that transcends testaments, Jesus is the precious rose of Sharon, the lily of the valleys, the bright morning Star, the Fairest of ten thousand to my soul.

Moving beyond the ancient practice of reading Song of Songs allegorically, however, one can affirm that there is another way of interpreting Song of Songs 2:1. In the larger context of Song of Songs 1:2–2:7, the young maiden in 2:1 is describing herself in relationship to her beloved. She is a wildflower, and her beloved is a stately apple tree of the forest (v. 3). This first section concludes with a lament expressed by the woman, which is repeated in 3:5, 5:8, and 8:3. John Bunn uses this phrase as a stackpole in piecing together an outline for the Song of Songs.[8]

The phrase "do not stir up or awaken love until it is ready!" provides an interesting opportunity for interpretation. Gledhill states that this passage is used to put the brakes on the physical proceedings just as if someone had doused them with cold water, and the same implication is repeated again when the phrase reoccurs throughout the book.[9] John Bunn interprets this phrase as an ethical admonition to traditional views of sexuality expressed rightly only in the appropriate relationship of marriage.[10] He writes, "Love, regardless of its inherent simplicity, purity, fidelity, and singular commitment is doomed when practiced outside of acceptable social and religious boundaries. It becomes an affront to admissible norms, and pressures from established institutions will ultimately turn its dreams to dust."[11]

2:8–3:5

The young maiden describes her lover as a youthful gazelle or deer who is coming for her, "leaping upon the mountains" (v. 8). The Hebrew word for "gazelle" has a homonym that means "beauty." The play on words is perhaps intentional as just another way the beloved confirms her admiration for her lover. Verses 11-13 announce the demise of winter and the arrival of spring. All is right in the world once again.

The male lover responds in 2:14-15. The lover compels an audience with his beloved. Verse 15 is problematic for interpreters. The meaning is unclear and appears to be taken out of context. Is this the remnant of another poem? Is it simply part of an idiomatic expression that is now lost due to the distance of time and space between the world of the author and our world today? Though commentators try, there is no general consensus on this verse, including the issue of who is speaking. Is it the lover? Is it the beloved?

In 2:16–3:5 the young maiden once again affirms her love for her lover and instigates a search for him. The Hebrew words *dodi li v`ani lo* are beautiful words of affirmation of mutual love and affection: "My beloved is mine and I am his." As a professor of Old Testament and Hebrew language at a small Christian university, I often entertain requests to aid people in search for the proper form of Hebrew to be used as a tattoo. These requests come for all types of reasons. A student has a personal breakthrough and wants to affirm the words of a verse that has proven instrumental in their development. Someone loses a loved one and wants to permanently remind themselves of their loved one with a lasting reminder. But by far the most commonly asked for Hebrew tattoo includes these words from Song of Songs 2:16. Once again, this section ends with the warning of v. 5: "Do not stir up or awaken love until it is ready!"

3:6–5:1

The careful reader will begin to notice the eclectic nature of the text beginning in 3:6. Someone is being praised as smelling nice and coming in from the desert? But who is this person? This verse seems unrelated to what comes before it or to what follows it. Because of such appearances, many scholars maintain that Song of Songs is some type of collection of love poetry. Is this the praise of the man for the woman, or the woman for the man? Is it spoken of by the daughters of Jerusalem mentioned in v. 5? Does it refer to what follows in vv. 7-11?[12]

Solomon's wedding carriage is the focus of Song of Songs 3:7-11. This passage is the only place in the book where the attention is directly focused on Solomon, who is mentioned by name in vv. 7, 9, and 11. The passage describes a royal entourage on one of Solomon's wedding days. As the reader we are not told which of the 700 wives this particular wedding was for. But it must have been a significant event. Sixty warriors serve as military escort for the royal carriage. Verses 8-10 focus on describing the royal carriage. It was made of cedar from Lebanon, silver, gold, and purple upholstery whose placement in the carriage is credited to the daughters of Jerusalem. The passage closes with a call to the daughters of Zion to offer their congratulatory statements to the king.

A beautiful description of the physical qualities of the women offered by the man comprises Song of Songs 4:1-7. When taken literally, one is left with a grotesque image. But we can only imagine that this was high praise in the culture and times of its day. Many of you have seen literal pictures drawn from this passage and what it actually looks like. It is quite amusing indeed. I dare not say to my wife that her hair is like a flock of goats, but perhaps in a culture replete with traveling flocks and nomadic people, this was better than it sounds today!

An invitation is offered from the man to the woman to escape in v. 8. Once again, the text changes abruptly from the description of the beloved, ending in v. 7. The woman, called "my bride" (4:8a), is urged to leave Lebanon and to travel safely past the den of the lion and snares of the leopard. Further description of their mutual love is witnessed in vv. 9-16. The invitation is offered to the man from the women in 4:16 and is accepted as complete in 5:1. These verses are filled with euphemisms, speaking of consummation of their mutual love for each other. The language is rich and beautiful. The man speaks with thankfulness as he has "come to my garden," "[gathered] my myrrh with my spice," "[eaten] my honeycomb with my honey," and "[drunk] my wine with my milk." Indeed, 5:1 is a rich description of the fulfillment of their love for each other.

5:2–6:3

This is the longest single love poem in the collection of love poetry of Song of Songs. It details the woman's search for her lover and her dialogue with the daughters of Jerusalem. The poem begins with the torment of the woman waiting for the arrival of her lover. She finally hears him stirring at the door, only to open the door and discover that he isn't there. The woman searches for her lover in the streets and is abused by the city watchmen in v. 7, recalling, "They beat me, they wounded me, they took away my mantle." In v. 8 the woman calls upon the daughters of Jerusalem to aid her in her quest to find her lover.

Like the description of the woman in chapter 4, the woman offers a detailed description of the man in 5:10-16. In poetic language the beloved describes her lover in strong, vivid terms. The description offered here is closer to a description of a man in a modern love poem than the imagery used previously of the woman. Who wouldn't want to be described in the following ways: "arms are rounded gold" (v. 14a), "body is ivory work" (v. 14b), or "legs are alabaster columns" (v. 15)? Heart, be still! The man is described as very handsome, even majestic.

The daughters of Jerusalem ask the woman to enlighten them upon the direction the man has traveled in 6:1. The woman responds with her confidence in her lover: "I am my beloved's and my beloved is mine" (v. 3). You can't blame the daughters of Jerusalem for trying to find this man, given the description just set before them in 5:10-17!

6:4–8:4

In 6:4 the man reappears in the text, praising the attributes of his beloved. Verses 4-9 are similar to what has already been discussed in 4:1-7. The lover compares the maiden to the cities of Tirzah and Jerusalem in v. 4. Tirzah served as the original capital in the northern kingdom of Israel before it was moved to Samaria (1 Kgs 16). Jerusalem became the capital of Judah and all of Israel during the reign of David when he captured the ancient city of Jebus, renaming it Jerusalem, and moved the capital from Hebron to Jerusalem (see 2 Sam 5). It may seem odd to today's reader to compare the attributes of a woman to a city, but these were not ordinary cities even in their day. These cities served as the respective capitals of their day, as places of wonder and amusement for the people of Israel and Judah. They also symbolized power and security for the people. On a side note, the references to Tirzah and Jerusalem can be seen as an anachronism for those holding to Solomon as the author of Song of Songs. Tirzah did not become the capital of Israel until Solomon had passed away, around the year 922 BCE.

The physical attributes of the woman are also addressed in 7:1-8. Songs of Songs 6:4–8:4 once again portrays the affection between the man and woman in poetic terms as they express their mutual love and admiration for each other. In 6:13 the woman apparently exits as the choir pleads, "Return, return, O Shulammite! Return, return, that we may look upon you!" Song of Songs 8:4 ends with the recurring refrain found throughout the work: "Do not stir up or awaken love until it is ready!"

8:5-14

No general consensus exists in the interpretation of the final section of Song of Songs. Roland Murphy credits this section as the best example of an "anthology" of love poems found in Song of Songs.[13] John Bunn offers the heading "the unique powers of love" for 8:5-14. Bunn writes, "In this, the climax of the book, the full force of its ethical implications become clear. The author delicately, but forcefully shows the destructive nature of love which circumvents the dimension of acceptable Israelite religious morality."[14] Indeed, 8:5-14 does seem to be a collection of fragmented lyrical poems speaking to the theme of the power of love.

In vv. 8-10 the younger woman is described before she has reached an age of maturation. She is protected and cared for until she can decide how to proceed with the care of her flowering. In v. 10a the woman responds, "I was a wall, and my breasts were like towers." She has reached maturity. She claims her independence in determining how she will express herself as a sexual being. The poem recounts, "My vineyard, my very own, is for myself" (v. 12). As witnessed throughout the book, the woman has decided upon the one who is to be her lover, and their mutual commitment has reached its point of consummation. The book ends with a call from the man to hear the woman's voice and the woman asking to be carried away.

Conclusion

Song of Songs is a wonderful diversion from the religious history, intrigue, or laments of suffering found throughout much of the Old Testament. Whether viewed as a solitary poem of love between Solomon and a wife/concubine or as a collection of love poetry, it offers a beautiful view of human love and its expression through human sexuality. We are created as sexual beings, and our sexuality can be redeemed as healthy and sacred. Song of Songs is an attempt at reclaiming human love and sexuality as a holy and sacred part of the creation of humanity. As a collection of love poetry, much of the book probably hearkens back to poems or hymns that were used for weddings or sacred ceremonies in ancient Israel.

In our culture, the sacredness of sexuality has been lost almost completely. Expressions of sexuality can be found in multiple forms through our world today. What is missing is the connection of this expressed sexuality with a sense of sacredness or otherness that is described in the book of Song of Songs. While many weddings still occur in beautiful cathedrals or churches, many times these places are used only because of their ascetic adornment and not as a place where people are cognizant of uttering vows of faithfulness before Almighty God. As a culture, we have settled for a cheap substitute of what God has created in the joy of sexuality. Human sexuality was created to be a lifestyle of intimacy and love to be enjoyed between a couple in the bonds of marriage. Is this an old-fashioned, outdated view? Probably so, but this view of marriage is the view that we find repeatedly throughout the Bible as the first institution God created.

For Further Reading

Bunn, John T. "Song of Songs." *The Broadman Bible Commentary*, vol. 5. Nashville: Broadman Press, 1971.

Gledhill, Tom. *The Message of the Song of Songs*. The Bible Speaks Today. Leicester, England: InterVarsity Press, 1994.

Matthews, Victor H. and James C. Moyer. *The Old Testament: Text and Context*. Peabody MA: Hendrickson Publishers, 1997.

Murphy, Roland. *The Song of Songs*. Hermeneia Commentary. Minneapolis: Fortress Press, 1990.

Soggin, J. Alberto. *Introduction to the Old Testament*. The Old Testament Library. Philadelphia: Westminster Press, 1989.

West, James King. *Introduction to the Old Testament*. New York: Macmillan Publishing Company, 1981.

Notes

[1] James King West, *Introduction to the Old Testament* (New York: Macmillan Publishing Company, 1981) 462.

[2] Frank Charles Thompson, ed., *The Thompson Chain-Reference Bible* (Indianapolis: B. B Kirkbride Bible Co., Inc., 1982) 643.

[3] West, *Introduction to the Old Testament*, 463.

[4] Tom Gledhill, *The Message of the Song of Songs*, The Bible Speaks Today (Leicester, England: InterVarsity Press, 1994).

[5] See the editorial uses of "beloved" and "lover" throughout the text of Song of Songs in the New International Version.

[6] Gledhill, *The Message of the Song of Songs*, 103.

[7] Words by Charles W. Fry, 1881, in *Celebrating Grace Hymnal*, ed. John E. Simons (Macon GA: Celebrating Grace, Inc., 2010).

[8] John T. Bunn, "Song of Songs," in *The Broadman Bible Commentary*, vol. 5 (Nashville: Broadman Press, 1971) 136.

[9] Gledhill, *The Message of the Song of Songs*, 128.

[10] Bunn, "Song of Songs," 136.

[11] Ibid.

[12] For a full discussion of this verse and the question of who is speaking, see Gledhill, *The Message of the Song of Songs*, 148–49.

[13] Roland Murphy, *The Song of Songs*, Hermeneia Commentary (Minneapolis: Fortress Press, 1990) 195.

[14] Bunn, "Song of Songs," 147.

Chapter 11

Esther

The story of Esther has provided source material for several movies in the late twentieth and early twenty-first centuries. Joan Collins starred in *Esther and the King*, directed by Raoul Walsh and Maria Bava in 1960. A made-for-television movie titled *Esther* aired in 1999, directed by Raffaele Mertes. Bollywood joined the queue of movies centering on Queen Esther in 2006 with *One Night with the King*, directed by Michael O. Sajbel. David A. R. White directed *The Book of Esther*, which was released in 2013. As demonstrated by these relatively recent productions, the story of Esther has a timeless quality, speaking to multiple generations, time periods, nationalities, and cultures. It is a story filled with intrigue, reversal of fortune, and courage, and it features powerful heroines at its center.

The book of Esther found within the collection named the *Megilloth*, a collection of five festal scrolls in the Hebrew Bible, has an interesting journey in its inclusion in the canon of the Old Testament Scripture. The word "God" never appears in the book of Esther. Faith, however, is oozing from every page of the work. The two principal characters in the book, Esther and Mordecai, demonstrate a passion for the perseverance of their Jewish heritage and faith. No portion of the book of Esther has been discovered among the many Qumran texts, better known as the Dead Sea Scrolls. The book of Esther appears to be the recording of an etiological story describing the origin of the celebration of Purim among the Jewish community. It is reported that Martin Luther had a notable disdain for the book of Esther, saying "it Judaized too much."[1] Yet in spite of these concerns, Esther continues to be a source of interest and hope for a variety of readers, both Jewish and non-Jewish alike.

A separate Greek version of Esther is believed to have been translated from the canonical Hebrew version in the second or first century BCE. The Greek translation adds 107 verses to the story. These additions generally give credit to a more conventional theological understanding of divine intervention than is present in the Hebrew version of Esther. There are six main additions to the story. The first addition describes a dream of Mordecai and his discovery of a plot leveled against the king (11:2-12; 12:1-6). The second addition adds the words of the royal decree against the Jews by Haman (13:1-7). The third addition contains the individual prayers of Mordecai and Esther (13:8-18; 14:1-19). The fourth addition describes the encounter of Esther as she appears unannounced before the king (15:4-9). The fifth addition is the royal edict uttered by Mordecai targeted against the previous edict offered Haman (16:1-24). The final addition is an extended version of Mordecai's dream (10:4-13). The word "Lord" or "God" appears over fifty times in the Greek additions to the book of Esther, perhaps hoping to make the story more palatable to its more conservative nationalistic readers in the Jewish faith, thereby making the theology of the book of Esther more explicitly orthodox.

The book of Esther shares the story of two powerful women, surviving in a harshly patriarchal culture, who demonstrate their power and authority in different ways. Queen Vashti refuses to be paraded as "eye candy" for her husband King Xerxes' pleasure and loses her position as the queen. Her refusal to be treated as simply the possession of the king is a bold move for a woman in the ancient world. Esther, or Hadassah in Hebrew,[2] finds her voice in more subtle ways than direct defiance. She moves indirectly toward the goal she wishes to achieve. She moves slowly, but with direct intent in working for the deliverance of her people from the wicked pogrom about to be implemented by Haman and the Persians against the Jewish people in Persia. These stories about women are only part of the story of Esther. The book itself provides the background and storyline for the celebration of the Jewish festival of Purim. The book also concludes with the Jewish people in Persia exacting revenge on their enemies, resulting in the deaths of over 75,000 people at the hands of the Jews. For a people who have suffered many such pogroms over the centuries, the story of Esther provides a theme of resounding hope and payback for a people who have frequently suffered at the hands of others based on the issues of race and ethnicity.

Some scholars have suggested the story of Esther is the remnant of an ancient Mesopotamian myth focusing upon the chief gods in Babylon, Ishtar and Marduk. These scholars argue the names Esther and Mordacai are derived from the names Ishtar and Marduk and demonstrate the secularization of this story and its association with an ancient festival known in Esther as Purim.[3] The word *Pur* is an Akkadian word that means "lot," as in the casting of lots.[4] The `*im* ending added to the word *Pur* is the plural ending in Hebrew, thus giving the reader the word *Purim*, or "lots." The word is first used in Esther 3:7, referring to the manner used by Haman in determining what day to extinguish the Jewish people: "In the first month, which is the month of Nisan, in the twelfth year of King Ahasuerus, they cast Pur—which means 'the lot'—before Haman for the day and for the month, and the lot fell on the thirteenth day of the twelfth month, which is the month of Adar." Purim today is celebrated in the winter months of late February or early March. It is a two-day festival commemorating the deliverance of the Jewish people by Queen Esther as told in this story. I have had the privilege of being in modern Israel on a couple occasions while Purim was being celebrated. Most recently, I witnessed a parade in honor of the Purim festival in Beth-Shan, with all the children dressed up in a variety of costumes. While in Jerusalem at the ancient site of the city of David, I photographed a young Israeli woman dressed up as a cat woman while working at the service desk at that location. It is a festive holiday for a people celebrating a time when the tables were turned and the Jewish people were able to take vengeance upon their enemies.

The author of this work is never identified in the book. Esther is a rare example of a book that tradition has not assigned a possible author for its writing. We simply do not know who wrote this book. It can be inferred that the writer was a Jew, probably part of the diaspora of the Jewish people, perhaps living somewhere in the east in the Mesopotamian region.**5** The activity of the book transpires during the reign of Ahasuerus (Xerxes I, 486–465 BCE), king of Persia, as stated in Esther 1:1. The book also claims that Mordecai, the cousin of Esther, was carried off into the exile along with King Jehoiachin (Esth 2:5-7). Jehoiachin was taken into Babylonian captivity in 598 BCE, which would make Mordecai at least 110–120 years of age when this story purportedly takes place. Most scholars ascribe a much later date to the writing of Esther than the time of the reign of Xerxes. A date of 300 to 50 BCE is generally agreed upon by the scholarly community. This late date affirms the omission by the Qumran community of Esther and the omission of either Mordecai or Esther from the famous roll call of Jewish heroes of faith recorded in the book of Ecclesiasticus, also known as the Wisdom of Sirach, written around 180 BCE.

The Texts of Esther
Esther 1:1–2:18

The story of Esther begins at Susa, described as the capital of Persia, though in reality it was the winter retreat of the kings. Ahasuerus, the Hebrew name for Xerxes I, the king of Persia, is sitting on his royal throne in the third year of his reign. Xerxes throws a banquet following a period where he has flaunted his great wealth and power. Esther 1:4-8 describes the opulence of this show of wealth by the king. Meanwhile,

Vashti, Xerxes' queen, also throws a banquet for the women of the royal palace. After seven days of feasting, Xerxes orders his eunuchs to bring Vashti to his banquet to display her beauty for all to see, but Vashti refuses the king's wishes. Vashti creates a crisis of law for the king. If the queen can refuse the wishes of the king, then what is to stop all women in the kingdom from refusing to obey the wishes of their husbands? The legal experts are consulted concerning a needed course of action. It is agreed upon that the king will proclaim an edict for Vashti to never again enter into the presence of the king and that her position as queen will be given to another. The edict is given. Verse 22 describes this event: "[Xerxes] sent letters to all the royal provinces, to every province in its own script and to every people in its own language, declaring that every man should be master in his own house." Jon Berquist writes, "The king's treatment of Vashti is foolish; he only loses when he acts. By connecting the king's foolishness to the mistreatment of women as objects, the narrator argues that such treatment of women is itself folly."**6**

Wow! Does this not seem eerily familiar to those of us who have lived in the world of Baptist politics throughout the last fifty years? With the changing of the Baptist Faith & Message in 2000, the official confessional document of beliefs adopted by the Southern Baptist Convention, it was decreed that the wife must graciously submit to her husband! Article XVIII on the family states, "A wife is to submit herself graciously to the servant leadership of her husband even as the church willingly submits to the headship of Christ."**7**

On the one hand isn't this exactly what the author of Ephesians 5:22 states when he says, "Wives, be subject to your husbands as you are to the Lord"? Yes, but it also ignores the verse preceding 5:22, which reads, "Be subject to one another out of reverence for Christ." The author of Ephesians has preempted this gender manipulation by stating up front that man and wife are to submit to each other! As Martin Luther King Jr. once called the Sunday morning 11:00 AM worship hour the most racially segregated hour in America, can we not also add that this hour has been the most gender-segregated hour as well? Now, I firmly believe in the autonomy of the local church to decide upon its own doctrine and polity. Yes, this includes the church's position on the issues of gender and leadership as well. But I wonder if Esther 1:22 isn't somewhat relevant and timely for many of our churches today that ultimately treat women as second-tier members of their church families. Vashti refuses the wishes of Xerxes. We do not know ultimately what became of Vashti, but at the very least she lost the title of queen and the favored hand of the king.

In contrast to Vashti, Esther comes onto the scene in Esther 2. Esther 2:5-7 describes Esther as "fair and beautiful," growing up as an orphan, raised by her cousin Mordecai in Susa. Mordecai is described as a Jew from the tribe of Benjamin who was part of one of the great deportations of the Israelites by Nebuchadnezzar and the Babylonians. Mordecai is also in a position of some power as a trusted advisor to the king. Esther is brought into the royal harem of Xerxes along with many other women from across the many Persian provinces. These women were being groomed in order to provide a pool for Xerxes to select his next queen. According to Esther 2:8-9, Esther gained favor with the eunuch Hegai, who was charged with watching over the king's harem. Following a lengthy preparation of twelve months of pampering, each girl would spend time with Xerxes, hoping to be chosen as the next queen of Persia. When Esther's time came, the text reads as if Xerxes was immediately smitten by her. A royal crown is placed upon her head, and Esther becomes the new queen. The text is careful to remind the reader that Esther has not disclosed her nationality as a Jewess to anyone. Esther heeds the words of Mordecai, keeping this knowledge a secret.

Esther 2:19–3:15

Mordecai is credited with discovering a plot against Xerxes and saving his life in Esther 2:19-23. Two of the king's officers had transpired to kill Xerxes, but Mordecai learned of this plot and alerted the king. The insertion of this side story to the larger drama plays a vital role later in the story. The two conspirators are hanged for their intentions to kill the king.

Throughout chapters 1 and 2 the reader is introduced to the hero and heroine of the story, Mordecai and Esther. In Esther 3 the villain, Haman, is introduced. The reader is introduced to Haman as a nobleman who is more honored above all the noble elite by Xerxes. The text describes the level of respect given Haman, saying that all the nobles knelt before him. All, that is, except Mordecai. The text does not reveal to the reader why Mordecai refuses to kneel before Haman. But Haman takes exception to this slight, setting a plan in motion by Haman to dispose of not only Mordecai, but also all of his kinsmen, the Jewish people living in Persia. Esther 3:7 says that lots (*purim*) were cast to determine when this act of genocide would occur. Haman approaches King Xerxes with his plan to exterminate the Jews, and the plan meets with the king's approval. A royal decree is proclaimed to this end with the date of the thirteenth day of the month of Adar selected as the appointed time of execution. Thus, seemingly without knowing it, King Xerxes has placed a sentence of death upon his wife's head. Esther is faced with a tough decision. Does she unveil her nationality and risk being placed with the other unfortunate Jews who are about to be put to death? Or does she keep quiet and hope that no one will discover her true heritage?

Esther 4:1–5:14

Mordecai, along with the Jewish people throughout Persia, begins a period of mourning for this unsettling news of Xerxes' decree assuring their execution. The story describes Mordecai practicing the ancient ritual of mourning by donning sackcloth clothes and covering himself in ashes. The Jewish people prayed, fasted, and mourned, crying out to the God of Israel, though the name "God" is never expressly mentioned within the pages of the text.

Mordecai sends word to Esther with the news of the decree, pleading with her to approach her husband to save her own people. Esther responds by reminding Mordecai of the dangers she faces if she goes unsummoned before the king. Verses 9-11 explain to the reader the seriousness of Mordecai's request. The unsummoned petitioner can be executed by coming before the king unless the king "holds out the golden scepter to someone" (v. 11). Mordecai proclaims a curse upon Esther if she refuses. Verse 14 records Mordecai's plea: "For if you keep silence at such a time as this, relief and deliverance will rise for the Jews from another quarter, but you and your father's family will perish. Who knows? Perhaps you have come to royal dignity for just such a time as this." Esther asks Mordecai and the Jewish people living in Persia to begin to fast and pray for her as she accepts the challenge laid before her. She exudes great faith, strength, and courage as she boldly proclaims in v. 16, "I will go to the king, though it is against the law. And if I perish, I perish." One of the reasons Esther has presented problems for theologians resides in this part of the story. Esther is about action. It is about acting on one's faith and not sitting back and allowing the events of life to presume upon the people. Much of the Old Testament rests upon the idea of God acting on behalf of the people, bringing forth deliverance or salvation. In the book of Esther, God is portrayed as hidden at best, perhaps somewhere behind the scenes, waiting for Mordecai and Esther to step out on faith and take action to deliver their people.

Esther takes action in chapter 5 when she goes before Xerxes. He extends the golden scepter, offering to grant any request she may make, up to half his kingdom. The door is wide open. Esther, however, does not take a direct path to her request. Instead, she diverts attention away from her true request by inviting Haman and Xerxes to a banquet in their honor. This pleases the king, and the banquet is held. Once again, Xerxes asks Esther to reveal what she wants before the king. Again, Esther acts indirectly. She invites Xerxes and Haman to another banquet the following day, where she will reveal her heart's intention before the king. Again, this request is granted. Meanwhile, following the banquet, Haman goes home filled with pride. He has been in the inner circle with a private banquet with both the king and the queen. This action is to be repeated tomorrow as well. He has arrived politically and socially. But once again, that fool Mordecai has slighted him on his journey home, refusing to kneel before him. His wife encourages him to build a high gallows and request Xerxes to hang Mordecai on those gallows the next day. Haman sets out to have the gallows built.

Have you ever received that text, email, or phone call requesting your presence with the president of the school, the CEO of the company, or the leader of any organization without much detail being given about the nature of the meeting? Our thoughts begin to wonder about the nature of this meeting. *Is a promotion near? Will I be recognized for all the hard work I have done? Just what is going on?* Perhaps you are a glass-half-empty type of person, and you begin to sweat it out with negative thoughts. *Just what have I done this time?* A few years ago, my oldest son worked for a local food distribution location, better known as a grocery store. He received word that the store manager wanted a private meeting with him. My son tells the story that the first words out of his mouth at the meeting went something like, "Sir, I am not sure what I have done this time, but whatever it was, I am really sorry." The manager laughed. He had brought my son into the meeting to let him know that he was very pleased with his work and with his demeanor with fellow employees and, most importantly, the customers. In fact, he was not in trouble, but was he was brought there to receive news of a small promotion within the store, along with a slight pay raise. But, oh, that time between the announcement of the meeting and the time when the meeting actually takes place can be filled with anxiety. Haman is excited. No telling what tomorrow may bring for him!

Esther 6:1–8:17

Esther 6 begins with Xerxes enduring a sleepless night. Is his spirit uneasy? He orders for the recorded history of his reign, described as the "Chronicles," to be read to him. The story of Mordecai's uncovering the plot on the king's life is part of the story read to Xerxes that night. The king asks his officials if Mordecai had been rewarded for his faithful duty. Having learned that Mordecai had not been rewarded, Xerxes determines to reward him. The next morning, the king asks if anyone has arrived in the royal court. Only Haman had arrived. He is brought before the king. Xerxes asks Haman for suggestions in honoring a faithful servant. This is it. All those days and years of faithful service are finally paying off! Yes, this is going to be a great day! Haman details a fitting honor. Haman says the person of honor should receive a royal robe worn by the king, be placed upon one of the king's royal horses, and be led through the streets of Susa with a proclamation, "Thus shall it be done for the man whom the king wishes to honor" (v. 9).

In a powerful reversal of fortunes, Xerxes commands Haman to find Mordecai and to fulfill these expressions of honor for him. Haman finds Mordecai, places the royal robe upon his back, helps him mount the king's horse, and parades him throughout the city with the accolades of honor. Haman is not pleased. This was to be his day, not Mordecai's! Upon returning home, Haman pours out his troubled heart to his wife and personal advisors. They remind him of the potential peril he now faces if he moves against Mordecai since he has received the favor of the king. The royal emissaries arrive and escort Haman to the private banquet with Esther and Xerxes.

Esther finally brings her plea for her people and for herself as a Jewess at the beginning of chapter 7. Esther asks the king to spare her life and the lives of her people from the proclamation ordering the extermination of the Jews in Persia. Xerxes demands to know who has led such an evil plot against his lovely queen. Esther points the finger across the table squarely in the direction of Haman. Haman is terrified and knows the outlook for him is deteriorating by the minute. When the king leaves the room, Haman throws himself upon the mercy of the queen, begging for his life. Xerxes returns to find Haman all over Esther, and he assumes the worst. Haman is taken outside and hung on the gallows Haman had personally prepared for Mordecai.

Esther

The reversal of fortune continues into Esther 8 as Queen Esther is given the estate of Haman. She, in turn, gives this estate to Mordecai. The king also takes the ring once worn by Haman as a symbol of his monarchial power and authority, placing it upon the hand of Mordecai. Esther once again approaches the king, pleading for leniency upon her people in light of the previous edict calling for a genocide to fall upon the Jews. Esther and Mordecai are ordered by the king to craft another edict to counteract the previous edict. After some thought, Esther and Mordecai deliver an edict that allows the Jews throughout the provinces of Persia to protect themselves against any armed forces that may try to carry out the previous edict written by Haman. As another sign of victory for Mordecai and Esther, Esther 8:15-17 mentions a joyous celebration breaking out among the Persian Jews for being spared this horrible fate ascribed to them by Haman.

Esther 9:1–10:3

What is described as a great picture of deliverance and salvation becomes troubling and vengeful in Esther 9:1-17. The author continues this story by detailing how the Jews went beyond their time of celebration and acted upon the edict of self-defense given by Mordecai and Esther and took this opportunity to kill over 75,000 Persians. Two days were set aside as days of revenge, the thirteenth and fourteenth of the month of Adar. The next day was established as a time of joyous celebration. A great two days to be a Jew in Persia, but an awful day to have been an enemy of the Jews in Persia. The remainder of Esther 9 and 10 serve as a didactic lesson, describing the background behind the celebration that has come to be known as Purim, celebrating the victory over the enemies of the Jewish people in Persia. The requirements for this celebration are credited to have been personally handed down by Queen Esther herself in Esther 9:29-32. The short conclusion of this version of Esther ends with the honoring of Mordecai, as he is described in 10:3, as the second in command in all of Persia.

As a person of faith who prefers the path of peace over the path of violence, I find Esther 9 to be quite troubling. It is one thing to pull for our two protagonists to survive the evil plot of Haman. It may even be okay to celebrate that Haman has found the same fate that he had prepared for Mordecai. But to read of the elimination of 75,000 people in response to the edict given by Esther and Mordecai is a disturbing turn of events. It is reminiscent of the days of conquest, when the Israelites were commanded to enter into the land of promise, destroying everyone and everything that stood before them (as instructed in Deut 7). One must bear in mind that the author is either intimately acquainted with the great deportations and the period of the exile, during which Jerusalem and the temple were destroyed and many lives were lost, or the author is mindful of the earlier history of one's people filled with stories of death and devastation. In this vein, here is one for the "good guys"!

Conclusion

Several years ago, my family and I were members of the Buies Creek First Baptist Church while I served as an assistant professor of religion at Campbell University. My wife served for a period of time as the part-time children's minister for this church. The children's ministry decided to offer a production of Esther for the church body. My oldest son played the role of Haman, and my middle son played the part of Mordecai! It made me a bit uneasy, as I could hear the hisses in the audience when Haman came upon the stage. I was equally uneasy by the rousing cheers for Mordecai when he entered the stage area. My oldest son, who is currently enrolled in divinity school, played the part of Haman with formidable glee! It causes me to reflect on the very heart of God when I remember this experience and relate it to the book of Esther. Must God not be pained when one son chooses to do evil and is demonized or even put to death? Are we all not God's children?

Esther is a great reminder to be careful about how we relate to each other. We must be careful in the things that we plan or wish on behalf of others. As the old adage goes, when we point a finger at others, we always have at least three fingers pointing right back at us. Proverbs 26:27 warns, "Whoever digs a pit will fall into it, and a stone will come back on the one who starts it rolling." The story of Esther warns us to leave judgment to the hands of a just and loving God.

For Further Reading

Berquist, Jon L. *Reclaiming Her Story: The Witness of Women in the Old Testament.* St. Louis: Chalice Press, 1992.
Bjornard, Reidar B. "Esther." *The Broadman Bible Commentary*, vol. 4 (Nashville: Broadman Press, 1971.
Matthews, Victor H. and James C. Moyer. *The Old Testament: Text and Context.* Peabody MA: Hendrickson Publishers, 1997.
Soggin, J. Alberto. *Introduction to the Old Testament.* The Old Testament Library. Philadelphia: Westminster Press, 1989.
West, James King. *Introduction to the Old Testament.* New York: Macmillan Publishing Company, 1981.
Yamauchi, Edwin M. *Persia and the Bible.* Grand Rapids: Baker Books, 1996.

Notes

[1] Riedar B. Bjornard, "Esther," in *The Broadman Bible Commentary*, vol. 4 (Nashville: Broadman Press, 1971) 1.

[2] See Esther 2:7.

[3] J. Alberto J. Soggin, *Introduction to the Old Testament*, The Old Testament Library (Philadelphia: Westminster Press, 1989) 469.

[4] Bjornard, "Esther," 3.

[5] Victor H. Matthews and James C. Moyer, *The Old Testament: Text and Context* (Peabody MA: Hendrickson Publishers, 1997) 244.

[6] Jon L. Berquist, *Reclaiming Her Story: The Witness of Women in the Old Testament* (St. Louis: Chalice Press, 1992) 157.

[7] Taken from Article XVIII, "The Family," in the *Baptist Faith & Message, 2000*, adopted by the Southern Baptist Convention.

Chapter 12

Daniel

The book of Daniel, like Jonah and Esther, is a writing for which there is little agreement on provenance, date of writing, or authorship. Each of these works has a rich history in the tradition of the Hebrew Bible. Scholars are divided about the time of writing of the book of Daniel, but they mostly agree that the book represents one of the most complete examples of apocalyptic writing found in the Hebrew Bible. Jonah continues to confound scholars with its simplicity and outward call for inclusion into the work of God in Israel's history. Whether a work of historical record or a children's story, the point of the work continues to remind us that the God of Israel is concerned with the well-being of all people, including our most hated enemies. Esther reminds its readers that God can use us in many different contexts when we are open to God's direction in our lives, even in the face of enemies who are actively working for our demise.

Apocalyptic literature became a dominant form of writing during the Greek occupation of Palestine in the second to first centuries BCE. Several Jewish books contained in the Jewish Apocrypha are very similar to what we find in the book of Daniel. The book of Tobit gives an account of a man from the tribe of Naphtali who is taken into captivity in the eighth century BCE by the Assyrian Shalmanezer. The book of Judith records the tale of Judith in the twelfth year of

Nebuchadnezzar. The book of 1 Esdras begins with the time of Josiah (640–609 BCE) and ends abruptly around the year of 398 BCE. The book of Daniel itself contains three additions that are believed to have originated in the second century BCE. Sixty-eight verses, often referred to as the Prayer of Azariah and the Three Young Men, are inserted between Daniel 3:23 and 3:24. The story of Susanna is recorded as chapter 13 of the book of Daniel in the Septuagint. Susanna tells the story of how a young Daniel saves Susanna from an evil plot hatched by two elders. Bel and the Dragon is the addition of forty-two verses to the end of chapter 12 found in Greek manuscripts.

The word "apocalyptic" comes from the Greek word *apokalupsis*, meaning "hidden" or "to be revealed." This style became a dominant form of writing during times of persecution or political dominance. The writer uses language that will have meaning for his or her readers, but will ultimately not be fully understood by someone outside of his or her community. It can be described as cryptic or coded language. If you understand how to decipher the texts properly, you can understand clearly the message contained in the text. This was done for the protection of both the writer and the recipients of the texts. Other apocalyptic texts are located in the Hebrew Bible in Isaiah 24–27, often called the "Little Apocalypse"; Ezekiel 38–39; Zechariah 1:7–6:8; and Joel 2:1-11. Daniel 7–12, especially, gives evidence of an apocalyptic character.

A dominant theme of the theology of apocalyptic literature depicts the current age of world history giving way to God's final age—an age when wrongs are righted and justice reigns supreme. Apocalyptic writing is often presented with visions, strange symbolic acts, numerology, and the appearance of divine messengers or angelic beings. The authorship of these works is largely pseudonymous but is often ascribed to a well-known figure in the past, giving the text greater authority or credibility with its readership. This type of writing is usually written as a word of encouragement to those who are suffering at the hands of an oppressor, offering words of hope for those who are trying to sustain their faith during the present trial. For those who are in danger of death, it often points the

DANIEL

hearers toward the promise of a resurrection of life beyond the grave that will be worth their tribulation or trial. In the "Little Apocalypse" located in Isaiah 24–27, we find two references to a resurrection in 25:7-8 and 26:19. Daniel 12:2 records, "Multitudes who sleep in the dust of the earth will awake: some to everlasting life, others to shame and everlasting contempt" (NIV). This emphasis on an afterlife is believed to be a relatively late development in Jewish theology.

The language of Daniel is somewhat unique in the Hebrew Bible. Daniel is divided into larger sections written in Hebrew and Aramaic. Aramaic is a language that developed in the exilic time and beyond, taking Hebrew letters but developing its own cognates, alternative conjugations for verb forms, and even a variation in expressing the definite article. It is very closely related to the Hebrew language of the Hebrew Bible, but it is also distinctive. It was the unofficial language of the Jewish community during the ministry of Jesus in the first century CE. Daniel 1:1–2:4a and 8:1–12:13 are written in Hebrew; chapters 2:4b–7:28 are written in Aramaic. It is unknown why the book of Daniel is preserved in this fashion. Scholars also identify various Persian expressions and a few Greek terms scattered throughout the text of Daniel. The Greek Septuagint and the Latin Vulgate place the book of Daniel in the collection of the prophets, but the Hebrew Bible places Daniel among the *Ketuvim*, or the Writings, following the book of Esther.

Very little is known about the character of Daniel except from this book bearing his name. Rabbinic tradition ascribes Daniel as part of the royal line as a descendant of Zedekiah. According to Daniel 1:21 and 10:1, Daniel served as a government official until the third year of the reign of Cyrus, approximately 536 BCE. The name "Danel" is a repeated figure in ancient Near Eastern literature. The Tale of Aqhat records the name Danel as a righteous man of ancient times. The name Danel also appears in the text of Ezekiel 14:14 and 14:20 as a revered righteous man of old in the order of Noah and Job.

The book of Daniel is often divided by its content between chapters 1–6 and 7–12. Daniel 1–6 deals with the exploits of

Daniel and his three friends and their interaction with the leaders of the Babylonian and Persian governments during the sixth century BCE. It is written in third person in the form of a biography, marked by stories about Daniel, Shadrach, Meshach, Abednego, and the king.

Daniel 7–12 focuses on the period of 175–164 BCE, during the time of the Maccabean revolt, describing the confrontation of the Jewish people in Palestine with Antiochus IV Epiphanes, who desecrated the Jewish temple, leading to the Maccabean revolt. Daniel 12:11 records "the abomination that causes desolation," interpreted by many scholars today as the act of sacrificing a pig on the altar in the temple of Jerusalem in 175 BCE. This section is written as autobiography and is apocalyptic in nature.

When taken together, the reader can hear the words of encouragement during the time of the Maccabean revolt taken from the lives of Daniel and his friends. If God can rescue Daniel from the lions' den and his friends from the fiery furnace, then the God of Israel can surely save the followers of the Maccabees during this armed conflict. And even if they perish, they will be rewarded by the hope of a resurrection, as promised in Daniel 12:1-4.

The Texts of Daniel

The book of Daniel is easily divided into two units. Daniel 1–6 details the story of four friends who are taken into captivity in Babylon. The stories all center on the desire of the Babylonians and later Persians to "reprogram" the youth of Israel into the cultural norms of Babylon and Persia. The four friends, who are known as Daniel, Hananiah, Mishael, and Azariah in Hebrew, are all given new names by their captors: Belteshazzar, Shadrach, Meshach, and Abednego, respectively. These stories focus on the four friends' ability to remain loyal to their religious convictions in spite of the threat of personal loss.

Daniel 7–12 represents the best example of apocalyptic literature in the Hebrew Bible. The stories of the latter part of

Daniel

Daniel focus on life during the persecution the Jewish people were enduring at the hands of Antiochus IV around 170 BCE. The texts call the people to maintain their steadfastness to their faith like Daniel and his three friends had done during the exilic period. The nature of the apocalyptic literature calls for a future hope. Though times were hard, there remained hope for those who maintained their faith in the God of Israel.

Daniel and His Three Friends, 1–6

Six stories about Daniel and his friends comprise the first six chapters of Daniel. The Babylonian captivity in the sixth century BCE provides the setting for these stories. It is unknown if these stories were handed down in some written tradition before being brought together in the second century BCE or if these stories were penned from an oral tradition dating back to the exilic period. Of course, it is also plausible that these stories are the literary creations of a second-century author using historical figures from the exile to deliver the intended message.

Daniel 1

The reader is introduced to the adventures of Daniel and his three friends in Daniel 1. The first verse is troublesome from a historical standpoint. It dates the beginning of the first deportations from Israel to Babylon by Nebuchadnezzar as taking place in the "third year of the reign of King Jehoiakim," or 606–605 BCE. Historically, the first major deportation took place in 598 BCE, following the death of Jehoiakim, when Jehoicahin, Jehoiakim's successor, is taken away into captivity. Daniel, along with his three friends, is among the elite of Israel, who were taken away into Babylon.

The first temptation of adapting to Babylonian culture and religion comes with the issue of dietary concerns. The healthiest among the captives are placed under the care of Ashpenaz, the chief of the king's officials, to be trained to be used in the king's court. The young men are offered the choicest food and drink the king has to offer. Daniel and his three friends refuse to eat the rich foods from the king's table and instead eat only vegetables and drink only water. Ashpenaz becomes concerned because he knows if the boys become weak or suffer because of lack of nutrition, he will pay the price for this development. Daniel strikes a deal with Ashpenaz to allow them to eat in their own manner for ten days and then to compare Daniel and friends to the other men who have eaten the rich food. After ten days, Daniel and his friends appear healthier than those who ate the rich foods. Needless to say, Ashpenaz places all the captives on the same dietary track as Daniel and his friends. Beneath the words of this text is more than just the physical well-being of Daniel and his friends. Their kosher, or "clean," manner of eating allowed them to keep the dietary laws they were taught to eat from the religious laws of their forefathers. Chapter 1 ends by stating that Daniel and his friends began to prosper in their standing with their captors.

Daniel 2

Nebuchadnezzar is plagued by a disturbing dream in Daniel 2. Daniel 2:1 states the dream took place in the second year of Nebuchadnezzar's reign. In Daniel 1:5 and 1:18, however, the texts state that Daniel and his three friends have served for at least three years in the king's service at this time. These types of inconsistent details highlight the belief that these stories are not part of an earlier contiguous narrative, but rather are brought together in Daniel like Polaroid snapshots, detailing separate stories of Daniel and his three friends. The king calls for his wise men, described as "magicians, enchanters, sorcerers," to first tell the king what he had seen in his dream and second to interpret the dream for him. His royal wise men were perplexed. How could they possibly tell the king what he had dreamed? The king also upped the ante on this group by saying they would be put to death if they were incorrect in recounting the specific details of the king's dream or in properly interpreting his dream. When the royal wise men are unable to comply with the king's wishes, he orders the execution of all the wise men of the royal court, including Daniel and his three friends.

When Daniel learns of the king's orders to execute these men and the basis for the execution, he volunteers to interpret the dream for the king on behalf of the royal wise men. He immediately calls upon his three friends to pray for him, asking God for divine intervention in this predicament. In the middle of the night, the author says that Daniel received divine intervention in the form of a vision. Daniel then goes to Nebuchadnezzar, pleads for mercy on behalf of the royal wise men, and proceeds to share with Nebuchadnezzar the content and the interpretation of his dream. Daniel explains to the king how he witnessed a giant statue with a head of gold. The head of gold represents four kingdoms. The head of gold is Nebuchadnezzar and the kingdom of Babylonia. The other three kingdoms are not explicitly identified in the text, but most probably relate to the kingdoms of Media, Persia, and Greece. These three kingdoms represent the transition from Babylon to the proposed time of the writing of this document, near the time of the Maccabean revolt in the second century BCE. Daniel continues to say that after these four kingdoms have passed away, God will establish a kingdom that will never be destroyed. The original audience of this text, comprised of devout Jewish believers, would identify the nation of Israel as the implied kingdom of which Daniel speaks. These words find favor with the king, and Daniel and his three friends are rewarded with even greater positions within the kingdom.

Daniel 3

The third tale recorded in Daniel 3 tells one of the most famous stories in the book of Daniel, the story of the fiery furnace. These thirty verses tell of three men, Shadrach, Meshach, and Abednego, who refuse to bow before the pagan gods of Babylon even when faced with the threat of losing their own lives. Their courage comes from their utter dependence upon and obedience to the God of Israel and God's decrees. The story begins with King Nebuchadnezzar building a "golden statue whose height was sixty cubits and whose width was six cubits; he set it up on the plain of Dura." The king commands that when the music is played, everyone must fall and worship the image before them. Anyone who does not bow will be subject to being thrown into a "furnace of blazing fire" (v. 6). Some of Nebuchadnezzar's officials point the finger at Shadrach, Meshach, and Abednego as violating the king's orders to bow down before the giant statue. Furious with this news, Nebuchadnezzar appeals to these three men to simply bow at the appointed time or forfeit their lives in the fire. The response by the three to this request is recorded in vv. 17-18: "If our God whom we serve is able to deliver us from the furnace of blazing fire and out of your hand, O king, let him deliver us. But if not, be it known to you, O king, that we will not serve your gods and we will not worship the golden statue that you have set up." Shadrach, Meshach, and Abednego gave witness that it was better to die being obedient to the God of Israel than to live a life of disobedience. They indeed refused to bow and were all cast into the fire.

The Greek version of Daniel adds what has come to be known as the Prayer of Azariah and the Three Young Men, following v. 23, a prayer asking God for help. It also gives a few details of what transpires in the furnace and concludes with words of praise for God's deliverance. To Nebuchadnezzar's amazement the men were unhurt by the flames. Their clothes were not singed, and remarkably they did not even smell like smoke, according to v. 27. Much has been written concerning the words of the king in v. 25: "But I see four men unbound, walking in the middle of the fire, and they are not hurt; and the fourth has the appearance of a god." In v. 28 the fourth man is identified as an angel who was sent by the God of Israel to rescue the men. The men are rewarded for their faithfulness. Nebuchadnezzar decrees that no one shall say anything against the God of these three men without stiff reprisal from the king. The king also promotes the three friends to a higher station of service. When read through the lens of the Maccabean revolt, this story proves to be very encouraging and uplifting. People were beginning to lose their lives by not bowing before the decrees of Antiochus IV. The passage of defiance credited to the three would have been viewed as a rallying cry among the rebellious of Israel. Our God is able to save, and even if not, we will not yield!

Daniel 4

The fourth story, found in Daniel 4, tells of another of Nebuchadnezzar's dreams, Daniel's subsequent interpretation, and the coming to fruition of the dream. This story is written in the form of a proclamation by the king, outlining why he offers praise to the God of the Israelites. Once again, Nebuchadnezzar has a dream. In this dream he shares that he has seen a large tree in the middle of the land. A messenger comes and proclaims the tree is to be cut down, but the stump is to remain in the ground. In two obscure verses, 15 and 16, the king says that one will be drenched with the "dew of heaven," and he will grow mad and live among the wild animals. Belteshazzar, or Daniel, offers his interpretation of this dream, stating that the tree represents Nebuchadnezzar. Daniel says that like the tree, the king will grow mad and be driven away from the people to live with the wild animals. The stump represents restoration that, months later, these things come to pass. Nebuchadnezzar grows mad, becoming like a wild animal, and is driven away from the people into the wild. Once the king repents and praises the God of Israel, he is once again restored. Some scholars suggest there is a parallel between Daniel 4 and the *Prayer of Nabonidus* discovered with the Qumran texts. Nabonidus is the last king of Babylon, who spent ten years away from the capital battling some type of affliction.[1]

Daniel 5

The mysterious writing on the wall is the heart of Daniel 5. In this story Nebuchadnezzar is no longer in the picture, but instead his reign has given way to King Belshazzar, who is said to be Nebuchadnezzar's son. In reality, Belshazzar was the son of Nabonidus. He reigned only in the absence of his father and was never actually crowned king of Babylon. In a show of arrogance and pride, the story tells that Belshazzar orders that the golden and silver goblets from the Jerusalem temple be brought so that his wives and concubines might drink from them. While the entourage consumed their drink, offering libations to the gods of silver and gold, a mysterious hand appears and begins writing on the wall. Four words are written: *mene, mene, tekel, parsin*. Though the meaning of these words is unclear, a general meaning appears to be something like: numbered, numbered, weighed, and divided.[2] In 5:26-28 Daniel once again interprets the meaning of this sign before the king. Daniel relates that the days of the reign of Belshazzar are numbered. The king has been weighed and found to be wanting, and his kingdom will become divided and given to the Medes and the Persians.

Daniel 6

The story of Daniel in the lions' den is the final story of Daniel and the three friends in Daniel 1–6. Once again back to the Polaroid snapshots, the reader is taken beyond the reigns of Nebuchadnezzar and Nabonidus; Darius is now on the throne. Daniel 5:31 describes Darius as "Darius the Mede," who took control of the kingdom of Babylon from Belshazzar. There is no record of a Darius the Mede ever reigning in Babylon, but three separate kings named Darius reigned in the Persian Empire.[3] The first Persian king who conquered Babylon and put an end to its reign as the dominant power in the region was Cyrus, the king of Persia, who is said to be king of the Medes and Persians. Once again, this lack of attention to historical details alerts the reader that the author of Daniel is not concerned with writing history for history's sake, but rather has a theological message intended for people who are enduring intense suffering and persecution, most likely during the time of the Maccabean revolt in the second century BCE.

Jealousy among the royal court turns its ugly head toward Daniel. The administrators try to find something to use against Daniel but are stymied in their endeavors, so they decide to use Daniel's commitment to the law of his God against him. They asked King Darius to declare it to be illegal to pray to any god or man for the next thirty days. The only exception is for the person to pray to King Darius himself. Daniel defies the king's order and continues to practice his daily routine of praying three times a day. The administrators bring Daniel's defiance to the king's attention. Though troubled by this development, the king nonetheless orders Daniel to be thrown in a den of lions, adding, "May your God, whom you faithfully serve, deliver you!" (v. 16). The next morning, the king awakens and makes his way to the lions' den, where he discovers that the lions have not had their way with Daniel. In turn, Darius orders those who had accused Daniel of misconduct to be thrown into the lions' den along with their families. Daniel is once again delivered from harm through his faith and trust in the God of his forefathers. Darius proclaims what the God of Israel has done for Daniel, and Daniel is rewarded openly for his faithfulness.

Each of these stories of Daniel and his three friends shares a common theme: God rewards faithfulness. The stories also remind the reader that the God of Israel is able to save from any circumstance, no matter how dire or how severe! This is a great message of hope and courage. If scholars are correct in their assessment of the time and place for the writing of Daniel, these words must have provided a great deal of hope and comfort for those who were standing up to Antiochus IV and his army during the Maccabean revolt. These messages are also timeless truths for all people who find themselves under the threat of persecution. God is able to save, but even if God does not choose to intervene with deliverance, faithfulness is always rewarded.

Help Is on the Way, 7–12

The remaining chapters of Daniel are steeped in the apocalyptic tradition popular in the second and first centuries BCE. The texts are filled with imagery that seems bizarre by today's standards. There is the appearance of angelic messengers and numeric references.[4] Throughout the second half of Daniel, the story is narrated by Daniel or by angelic beings, detailing God's victories over the conventions of humanity, including the rulers of men and their armies. The writer switches from the vantage point of third person, found throughout chapters 1–6, and now writes primarily in first person. Also, Daniel's three friends are not mentioned in the second half of the book. Throughout Daniel 7–12 a consistent message appears: The current age is evil, but help is on the way. In these texts the faithful are encouraged to remain true to their faith and to be hopeful that a better day is coming. Four primary visions dominate Daniel 7–12: the four beasts (ch. 7), the ram and the he-goat (ch. 8), the seventy years (ch. 9), and the last days (chs. 10–12).

Daniel 7

Daniel 7 begins back in the reign of Belshazzar, mentioned previously in Daniel 5. Daniel is now the one having the vision in the form of a dream. Daniel sees four great beasts emerging from the seas: a lion, a bear, a leopard, and a fourth beast unlike the others. Taken alongside Daniel 2 these four kingdoms are traditionally identified as the kingdoms between the setting of Daniel (the Babylonian Empire) and the writing of the words of Daniel (the Maccabean revolt). Therefore, the four kingdoms represent the Babylonians, the Medes, the Persians, and the Greeks. The little horn speaking boastful words is traditionally identified as Antiochus IV. While the first three beasts fade away, the fourth beast is destroyed by fire. The vision of the beasts is followed by the vision of one described by the term "son of man," a term used extensively in the book of Ezekiel. This figure is often identified as the messiah who is to come. Daniel seeks help in interpreting his dream. He is informed that the fourth beast will be removed by the Most High. The time of the reign of terror by the fourth beast will be approximately two and a half years, closely approximating the time of the terror of Antiochus IV from 167 to 164 BCE.

These words are words of encouragement to those faithful Jewish people who have been witness to the terror imposed upon them by Antiochus IV. Their religious practices have been interrupted. A pagan altar has been erected in the temple of Jerusalem, and they have witnessed the further desecration of the temple with the sacrificing of a pig inside their sacred temple. Daniel offers words of hope that these evil days will end. A brighter day is coming, filled with justice, when rulers of the earth will obey and live by the rules and laws of the Most High.

Daniel 8–9

Daniel entertains a vision of a ram and he-goat in Daniel 8, and once again the reign of Belshazzar serves as a backdrop for the recording of this vision. The ram and the male goat are identified in Daniel 8:20-21. The ram is identified as the kings of the Medes and Persians. The king of Greece is named as the male goat, with the large horn between its eyes identified as Greece's first king. Four prominent horns replace the large horn when it is broken off. History records that following the death of Alexander the Great, the king of Greece, his kingdom was divided into four separate provinces, ruled by Alexander's four principal generals: Macedonia and Greece, Asia Minor, Syria, and Egypt. Antiochus IV was over the area of Syria and Palestine during the time of the Maccabean conflict. The angel Gabriel appears in 8:16 to interpret this vision to Daniel. Daniel is immediately frightened by this appearance. The name Gabriel is a contraction of two Hebrew words, *Gibor El*, meaning "mighty warrior of God." Daniel is once again reassured that the plots of these evil kings will not prevail. These kings will be put to death by the one identified in 8:25b as the "Prince of princes." Gabriel assures Daniel that the little horn will be defeated, but not by human hands. God has not abandoned the people living under the oppression of Antiochus IV.

The people are to remain faithful to their God and God's law. God will deliver them.

Daniel 9 provides a lengthy interpretation of the term "seventy weeks" first revealed in Jeremiah 25:11-12 and 29:10 in reference to the exile. In Daniel 9 the term "seventy weeks" refers to the amount of time Israel will be oppressed. The setting for this scene has moved beyond the kingdom of Belshazzar to the time of Darius, now identified as the son of Xerxes, the Persian king. Daniel's prayer in vv. 4-19 affirms traditional Deuteronomistic or retribution theology. Jerusalem and the people deserve the judgment they have received through the atrocities of the exile and now the Seleucid ruler Antiochus IV, but Daniel pleads for God to be lenient on the people, asking for forgiveness on their behalf. In vv. 20-27 Daniel has another encounter with the angelic messenger Gabriel. Gabriel relates that the term "seventy weeks" actually refers to weeks of years or "490 years." Gabriel assures Daniel that the end of the reign of judgment is almost over. In terms of the recipients of Daniel's message, the writer is assuring his hearers that their wait is almost over. They must be faithful waiting for the Most High to deliver them from this time of oppression.

Daniel 10–12

Still another backdrop is offered for Daniel 10–12. The reader has been moved along to the time of Cyrus, king of Persia. Having prayed and fasted for three weeks, Daniel encounters an unidentified angelic being. The angel shares with Daniel that his cries for help have been heard, but that he was detained due to a conflict beyond the earthly realm until Michael, a chief angelic prince, came to his aid. Throughout Daniel 11 the angel gives an overview of the events, beginning with the time of Alexander the Great through the time of the Romans in Daniel 11:2-30.[5] Daniel provides a theological interpretation of the historical events, focusing on the time of the Ptolemaic and Seleucid control over Palestine, leading up to the time of Antiochus IV. Daniel also provides words of future hope. Daniel's hope does not lie with armed conflict, but rather with the salvation that can only come ultimately through the God of Israel. A recurring literary device is found in Daniel 11:7, 14, 20, 29, and 40. Each section begins with the refrain "in those times" or "at the time of the end."

The message of Daniel 1–11 is brought to a conclusion in Daniel 12. Daniel states that the long years of abandonment and persecution will soon be over. God will deliver those who have remained faithful to God. The Jews of the second century are encouraged to remain faithful to their religious heritage, apart from the Hellenistic culture that is being forcibly imposed upon them. Daniel reminds the people of the lordship of the God of Israel over all things, historical kings and rulers, angelic conflicts, and daily struggles. The concept of life after death is also introduced in Daniel 12:2: "Many of those who sleep in the dust of the earth shall awake, some to everlasting life, and some to shame and everlasting contempt." This developing concept of life beyond death first appears late in the development of the theology of Israel and would continue to be a topic of hot debate among Jewish religious leaders for years to follow. To those who are losing their lives as martyrs due to oppression, these words offer life-giving waters of hope. These springs of hope would also be particularly helpful for loved ones of those who were martyred for their faithfulness to the God of Israel. Daniel 12:13 ends with a word of blessing for Daniel, or the "author" of these words: "But you, go your way, and rest; you shall rise for your reward at the end of the days."

Conclusion

I will never forget my introduction to the apocalyptic literature of the Bible. As a youngster living in rural Oklahoma, my little country church would invite an evangelist/preacher from the big city of Tulsa every year to come and speak to our church. Let's just call him Pastor P. Pastor P would bring large charts with colorful images, outlining the events of the end times and last days. The promise of understanding the end times always drew a crowd! Daniel 7–12 was often the heart of the discussion and a key player in figuring out what was about to transpire in world history, according to Pastor P. These meetings were often followed with movies like *A Thief in the Night*, focusing on the theme of not being left behind, long before the Kirk Cameron phenomenon!

As a youngster, I was constantly barraged with the message that these apocalyptic images were simply a blueprint for the end times. If we could just find the hidden key, we could know and understand the events of our world and the world to come in preparation for the return of Christ and the coming kingdom. Later, as a student at Oklahoma Baptist University, Golden Gate Baptist Theological Seminary, and The Southern Baptist Theological Seminary, I was introduced to the larger field of studies in the area of apocalyptic literature. Imagine how freeing it is to know that while the apocalyptic literature does reinforce a better day to come for those who are faithful, we also have power for living in the midst of the tumult of today. When I discovered these texts as words of hope for real people facing real crises in their day, it opened up a whole new way of experiencing the Scripture. As a person of faith today, we don't need some hidden code to understand these apocalyptic texts. We simply need a heart of faith to know that like these people of old, God is still with us, working things to God's own end. Our deliverance is assured through faith in God.

For Further Reading

Blenkinsopp, Joseph. *A History of Prophecy in Israel*. Louisville: Westminster John Knox Press, 1996.

Goldingay, John E. *Daniel*. Word Biblical Commentary, vol. 30. Waco: Word Books, 1989.

Matthews, Victor H. and James C. Moyer. *The Old Testament: Text and Context*. Peabody MA: Hendrickson Publishers, 1997.

Owens, John Joseph. "Daniel." *The Broadman Bible Commentary*, vol. 6. Nashville: Broadman Press, 1971.

Pace, Sharon. *Daniel*. Smyth & Helwys Bible Commentary. Macon GA: Smyth & Helwys Publishing, 2008.
Reddish, Mitchell G. "Daniel." *The Prophets: Mercer Commentary on the Bible*, vol. 4. Macon GA: Mercer University Press, 1996.
Von Rad, Gerhard. *The Message of the Prophets*. San Francisco: HarperSanFrancisco, 1965.
Wallace, Ronald S. *The Message of Daniel: The Lord Is King*. The Bible Speaks Today. Leicester, England: InterVarsity Press, 1984.
West, James King. *Introduction to the Old Testament*. New York: Macmillan Publishing Company, 1981.

Notes

[1] Mitchell G. Reddish, "Daniel," in *The Prophets: Mercer Commentary on the Bible*, vol. 4 (Macon GA: Mercer University Press, 1996) 224–25.

[2] Ibid., 226.

[3] John Joseph Owens, "Daniel," in *The Broadman Bible Commentary*, vol. 6 (Nashville: Broadman Press, 1971) 411.

[4] Victor H. Matthews and James C. Moyer, *The Old Testament: Text and Context* (Peabody MA: Hendrickson Publishers, 1997) 257.

[5] For a good overview of the historical figures identified behind the language of Daniel 11:2-30, see Reddish, "Daniel," 233.

www.ingramcontent.com/pod-product-compliance
Lightning Source LLC
Chambersburg PA
CBHW071708090426
42738CB00009B/1713